HUMOROUS U.P. FISHING STORIES

From a Bonifide YOOPER!

By the U.P. Rabbit
Robert R. Hruska

Humorous U.P. Fishing Stories

First Edition: 2000
Copyright © 2000
ISBN # 0-9668265-1-5

Published by
McNaughton & Gunn, Inc.
960 Woodlawn Drive
Saline, Michigan 48176

All inquires should be addressed to:
Robert R. Hruska, Author
140 S. Birch Avenue
Gillett, Wisconsin 54124
Telephone: (920) 855-2996

Illustrations by:
Brian Fretig, Teacher, Sportsman, and Friend

No portion of this publication may be reproduced, reprinted, or otherwise copied for distribution purposes without the author's written permission.

Dedication

To my courageous and wonderful Daughter-in-law, Kathy, and my Grandson, Cal, who's characteristics and gestures at two years old, are a carbon copy of his Dad's when he was that age.

Table of Contents

Chapter   Page

1: A Fly-In Fishing Trip
    And The Last Can of Beans..............1
2: Spearing Northern With Bill.................11
3: Fishing Hayward Lake.......................16
4: Hard Luck Joe
    The Trout Fisherman....................21
5: An Unforgettable Character
    Frank....................................25
6: Grandpa Fred and the Plywood Boat.......32
7: A Wild Fishing Adventure...................38
8: Bass Fishing Among the Deadheads........51
9: Two Unforgettable Characters
    Willie & Billie............................56
10: We Almost Died!
    A Near-Disaster Fishing Experience...62
11: Bear Tracks!..66
12: Early Rainbow Run on the Huron River.......72
13: Smelt Fishing
    Where Have All the Smelt Gone?......77
14: An Unforgettable Character
    Joe St. John.............................82
15: Mosquitoes
    As Big As Humming Birds..............87
16: The Trout Camp.....................................91
17: The Day The Wolf Almost Got Joe.............97
18: Trout Stream Fishing With the Wood Ticks..101
19: An Unforgettable Character
    Italian Leonard..........................106
20: The Suspicious Fisherman's Wife.............110

21: Planning A Fly-In Fishing Trip
    (Some Trips Fly, Some Don't).........117
22: Trout Fishing With Roger
    And His New Wife…......................121
23: Some Favorite Fishing Spots……………...126

Goin' Fishin'

Sven, from up Minn-e-sota way, was going for his morning walk one day when he walked past Ole's house and saw a sign that said, "Boat for Sale." This confused Sven because he knew that Ole didn't own a boat, so he finally decided to go in and ask Ole about it. "Hey, Ole," said Sven, "I noticed da sign in your yard dat says, 'Boat for Sale,' but you don't even have a boat. All ya have is your ol' John Deere tractor and combine." Ole replied, "Yup, and they're boat for sale."

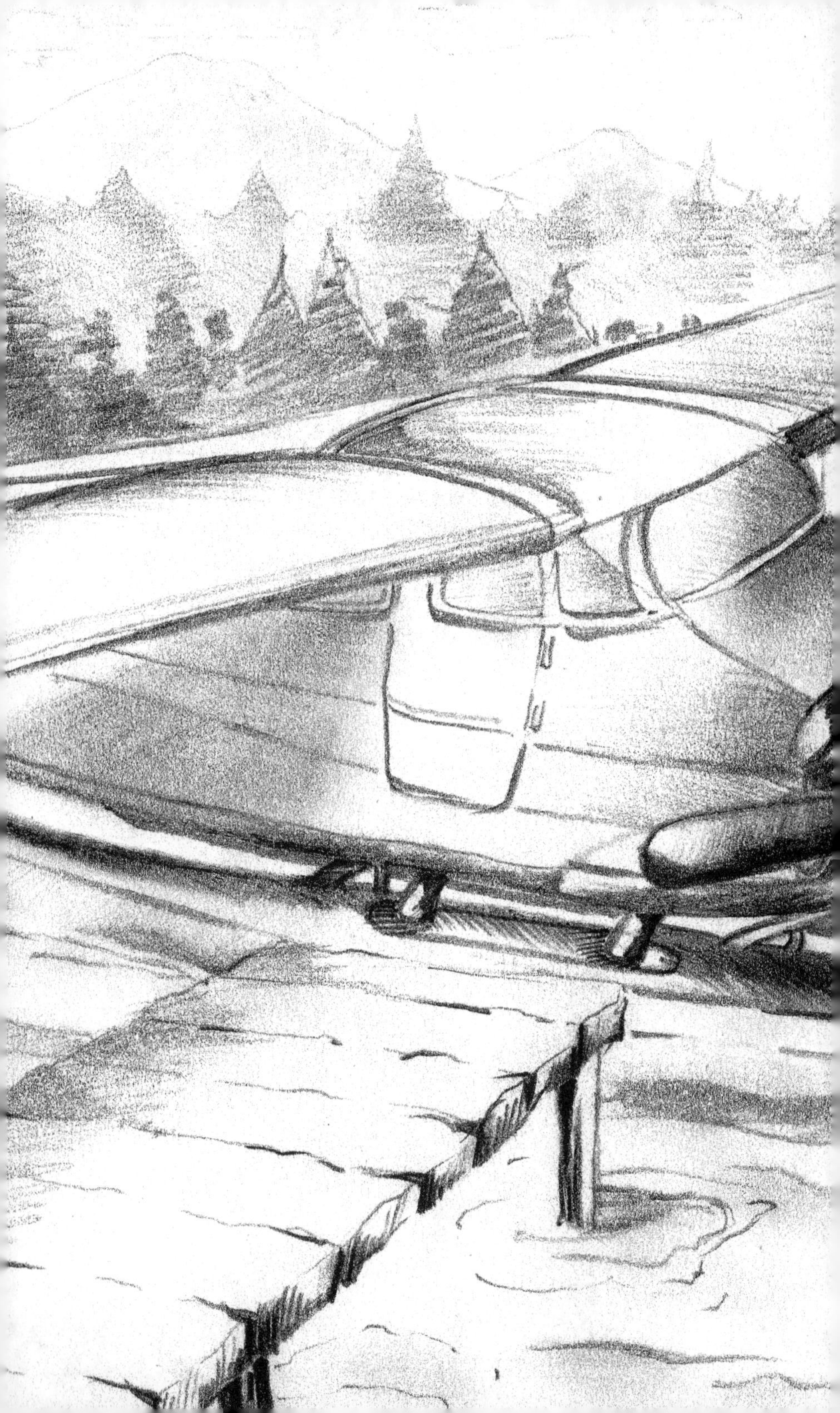

CHAPTER 1

A FLY-IN FISHING TRIP
AND THE LAST CAN OF BEANS

It was early fall and we were on our way to fish speckled trout in Canada. The lake we were going to, was excellent last year, for some very large trout. In fact, these were the biggest speckled trout that we ever caught in our lives.

A Fly-in trip to Moosejaw Lake. There is only one kind of fish in it. They are all speckled trout. To us fishermen, back home, speckled trout there are the same as our brook trout in the States. We discovered, some years ago, that a Fly-in trip can really provide some wonderful fishing. The Fly-in that we go on, can take a party of four people in the plane along with your week's supply of groceries, sleeping bags, fishing gear, and clothes.

There are no roads or trails coming into these lakes. The only access is with a pontoon plane. They use a DeHavliand Beaver. The engine (motor) on a Beaver is unbelievably loud and powerful. When it roars down the lake to take off, no one talks. No one could hear you anyway. Then, the pilot cuts back on it when it's leveled off in the air and the noise seems to cut in half.

Our biggest catch from last year was one 17½ incher. We caught close to a dozen 16½ inchers. The average size ran between 13 and 15 inches.

Picture yourself fishing on a Fly-in lake where the only fish in it are speckled trout.

Also a lake where there is only one cabin on the entire lake and one fishing party is allowed to fish it during the same week. There are also many weeks when this group of four lakes has no one fishing on them for weeks at a time. These trout are all red-bellied, native fish.

After the plane leaves, the only sounds you hear are lake loons, the wind, rapids between the lakes, and each other to talk to. It's lonely or peaceful. Depending upon your point of view.

We plan the trip right down to the pound of baggage that they allow us to fly in. The total four of us are allowed 400 pounds of baggage that has to include, your fishing gear, clothes and food for the week. We can successfully do this UNTIL we pick up our last guy, Dick. He has an extra aluminum cooler full of food that could weigh between 25-40 pounds. He cleans out his refrigerator and brings along everything that could spoil if he left it at home.

Everyone then gets on him, "What are you going to do with all of that stuff?" "Half of it looks spoiled already." "Why not leave it home?" "Did you ever think of giving it to a neighbor?" "That hamburger looks spoiled already."

He insists on taking it with. We hope that he might eat most of it on the way. He said, "I'm going to break up the hamburger and feed it to the fish. Besides, a dark banana like these with the dark spots on them are better for you than the green ones."

Dave looks at him with one eye closed. He figured, now here's a guy that we may be able to talk into taking the top bunk. Dick said, "And .... don't any of you get the idea of using my nice, aluminum cooler for a fish box in your boat. Bill told him, "If there's not two pails (one for each boat), we may need it for a fish box. Dick thought about that for a minute, and then said, "Well, only if there's no pail." Dave leaned over, smiling at me, and said "Hide the pail."

After driving 10 hours, we hoped that Dick ate most of that food that he brought. We arrived in Wawa, Canada and slowly got out of Dave's van. We walked into the Bristol Motel. We have stayed at this same motel for many years and the owner and his wife are like family. When they see us coming, they make two HUGE bowls of popcorn for us.

After a good night's sleep, we drive 12 miles to the Outfitter's Fly-in service. He's located there, 12 miles away from Lake Superior to avoid the constant morning fog that naturally develops from the cold water temperatures mixing with the warmer air near Lake Superior.

Last year, a cool, steady rain was coming down. The pilot said, "We have to wait out this rain, then I'll take you in. In the meantime, let's load the plane with your goods so we'll be ready."

We all carried our stuff to their scale by the dock. The dockhand would weigh most of it. I was watching him. As he got wetter from the now, heavy rain, he got less interested that everything was weighed on the scale. We gave him a can of LaBatts Canadian beer as he was working the scale. I don't know if it was the beer that helped or his disgust with working in the rain, but, he passed over that big, aluminum, heavy, extra-food, cooler, a case of beer, and two cases of pop that we had.

He said, "If you carry these items on your laps on the plane, I won't weigh them. It will count the same as "carry on" baggage on the bigger, commercial planes. They don't weigh that, so neither will I."

I was thinking, that saved us for paying for another trip to bring in the "overload" baggage. However, how did the PLANE know the difference of where those pounds of weight were? Either we were overloaded or we weren't. The plane's pontoons seemed to be noticeably sinking deeper into the water.

We gave the pilot a can of LaBatts too. He promised that he wouldn't drink it until he flew the trip first.

He told us, "Don't worry about a little extra weight guys. As long as I can clear the trees on the end of the lake, there, we'll have it made. When it's airborne, it's easy to fly."

I couldn't help but notice that he made the sign of the cross before he started the plane up. Either he was real religious or he knew something that we didn't know.

After the plane ran the whole length of that lake, the plane's pontoons broke free from the water. We cleared the treetops by what looked like 20 feet. I could see a squirrel jumping out of a tree to the ground. I guess its true. If you miss the trees by 2 feet or 200 feet, you still missed them.

After waiting for four hours, we're finally flying. It was foggy, drizzling a little, and we had to fly somewhat low to the ground as the pilot could fly by only what he could see. No instrument flying with these bush planes.

We were flying low. I looked out the window and couldn't believe what I saw…. I shouted to the pilot over the roar of the motor. "There's a mountain of rock about 100 yards off of this wing!" He said, "Don't worry. There's one off this wing too. I'm flying in a valley between them. If this fog doesn't lift, I'll have to turn back."

After another 20 minutes of low flying, I could see a lake below us. He circled the lake and landed in the middle of it. I knew it wasn't the lake we wanted to fish with a small, warm cabin included. I said, "Now what?" "We're going to sit out the fog, here. I can't see to fly back or to find your lake in this fog,' he commented. "Don't worry," he said. "This is standard procedure, up here. Did you notice that I fly a zigzag pattern keeping some lake under us? If we ever have a motor problem or fog problem like this one, we have a safe place to land."

He was well relaxed, like, hey, this is routine and a little patience waiting, and we'll be on our way. He pointed out of the right side window and said, "There's a high hill (like a mountain?) in that direction. When we can see it's top from the fog clearing, I'll take us up."

After a couple of hours of waiting and just before I thought we were going to run out of daylight, the fog did lift off of that huge hill. He took us up and was squinting to find some landmarks. I asked him what lake that was that we were on. "I don't know," he said. "There's all kinds of them down there." There were no cabins, roads, or any signs of people down there.

We touched down on our lake after about another 20 minutes of flying time. He made a very smooth landing and taxied up to the floating dock. He wanted to unload quickly so he could get out before the fog settled back in for the night.

I asked him, "What would you do if you couldn't find your way back?" "That's easy," he said. "I'd just land on another lake and spend the night in the plane." The life of a bush pilot…. No hurry, and it seemed like he was always, "Living on the Edge".
Don got out and was kissing the ground like you see the Pope doing on the news. I was thinking, maybe he's got a wild pilot, too.

We placed our sleeping bags onto the bunks, groceries on the shelves, threaded our fish poles and figured we'd still catch a few trout. We had two 14-foot boats with small motors and a whole lake for four guys. Don caught a 17½-inch speck, and we all caught some a little smaller. Did you ever think that anyone could get tired of eating fresh trout? One 16-inch fish was more than enough for one person to eat. They were fat and deep when they got over the 15-inch size.

The next day, we had a choice of doing a 10-20 minute portage to another chain of trout lakes with a boat and motor located there. We knew that this was the "best spot" to fish from a friend that made this trip before.

After breakfast, we set out to make the portage to these other lakes. We discovered that there was no good trail. No easy marks to follow. There was a fair sized stream flowing into the first lake from the ones we wanted to go to. One of us stayed within sight of the stream. No easy task, as, the brush was so thick near the stream that you could hear it, in most cases, rather than actually see it. The rest made small ½ circles from the stream to find the easiest way to walk uphill and without a trail, to the next lake.

We were walking, by choice, a good distance apart as it was hard going. All of a sudden, the first guy, Don, found fresh bear droppings where he was walking. I noticed immediately, there was no one straggling in the rear. Everyone was bunched up. It was hard to tell who was last. Like geese, alternating for the first place spot when they were flying.

Finally, we could see the new lake and the boats pulled up under the trees. We pulled them back into the water and Vic caught a trout immediately. He fishes in spots where common sense tells you there would be no fish and he catches them.

We caught our limits quickly. They were in the 13 to 16 inch range. What nice speckled trout! We were talking over, should we take a few extras to eat when we got in. It seemed at that same instant, a yellow pontoon plane came out of nowhere, circled us down low, and flew away. To see another plane or person in this fishing territory was highly unusual.

We were convinced that the game warden would now be waiting to visit us at our camp so we quit fishing. The portage back was quicker and easier. It was mostly down hill and we broke a few tree branches as trail markers.

When we got back to the cabin, no one was there but us. We have no idea whose plane came down to look us over.

We feasted on fried trout, beans, rye bread, pickles, and cottage fries. (Better known as American fries to us. In Canada, they, of course, are not called American fries.)

Where does the last can of beans come in? There is a "Camp Log" on a rafter there, in the cabin, where the fisherman can write in. There was a pretty desperate story in there about "The Last Can of Beans." I'll tell you about some of it. It was written by a fishing party that also used the camp. They didn't catch many fish and had to rely upon all of their groceries. They were "Fogged in" for some extra days. That means the fog settled in so thick that the plane couldn't fly in to pick them up. The rest is from the camp log:

First day fogged in: We are down on the groceries and the weather looks like we could be fogged in for at least another day. We have coffee, lake water, Mazola oil for cooking, and one can of beans left.

Second day fogged in: We are down on the groceries and the weather looks bad. We could be fogged in a lot longer. Our otherwise friendly group is now starting to act strangely. Ben drank some Mazola oil and now he's got the "Runs." Everyone has their eye on that last can of beans. No one wants to go to the lake and bring up water fearing the rest might eat the beans.

Being that I'm the group leader, I took it upon myself to hide the can of beans in case we have to stay a lot longer. Now, no one wants to shut their eyes when they got to sleep fearing someone will discover and eat the beans. One will even follow me to the "Out-house" when I go. Just so nothing happens to me, so he says. Everyone is getting hungrier and more irritated.
Ben said the Mazola oil wasn't bad if you drank it fast. Being that he still has the "Scoots," no one else seems moved to try it.

Third day fogged in: This has to be some kind of record. Three extra days without allowance for food. Because of the extra weight in the plane, you can only take in so much food. Someone is always going out on the porch and listening and watching for a plane. The fog is still thick. We made coffee again. Starting to use coffee grounds twice. No one wants that Mazola oil although, some are now starting to read its ingredients on the bottle. We opened the last can of beans today. The spoonfuls were carefully counted out to each one. We now know, what it means to go to bed hungry…..

Fourth day fogged in: Fog is lifting. 10:00 a.m. and we can see to the other end of the lake. Can hear a plane engine in the distance. Everyone ran out to the dock hoping it was for us. Plane came in at 10:15 a.m. I'm finishing this quickly as the others are loading the plane.

We talked the pilot out of a candy bar that he had. We're on our way out (10:45 a.m.) Thank God!

CHAPTER 2

SPEARING NORTHERN WITH BILL

Bill was a very nervous guy by nature. He was always in a hurry to go no where. He loved to hunt and fish but never had much patience to sit for a long time if it was necessary.

He was the kind of guy to continually rake his lawn in the summer or continually paint every room in his house in the winter. Each year, a different color.

A very nice guy, but if you tried to hold him still for 10 minutes, I think he'd explode! He's also my brother. He loved to go spearing northern during the winter spearing season. We made a fish shack, this one particular year, hauled it out onto the Menominee River, cut the original hole, and were ready for business.

I say, cut the original hole because anyone who ever did this sport knows it takes 1-2 hours to chisel out the refrozen, new ice in the hole each time. We had a chisel made from an old car drive shaft. It was about six feet long and three inches thick.

Bill was cutting the hole on the second fishing trip. I told him, he'd better attach the rope to his wrist (It was also attached to the chisel) so we wouldn't drop it in. "No, no, he said, "We're in a hurry. I'll have this done in nooooooo time, when…..PA-LUSH!! the chisel slipped out of his ice-coated gloves and went to the river's bottom. We borrowed another chisel, finished the hole, cleaned away the ice and there was our chisel, standing up right on the bottom of the river.

We quickly made another trip into town, got a long pole and wired it to a wooden-handled, metal rake. We lowered this by the chisel and hooked onto the metal ring on the chisel's top and pulled it up. Finally, we were squared away. When you are spear fishing, you can work the wooden decoy sometime for hours before ever seeing a fish. This was one of those times.

We were each sitting on seats on opposite sides of the hole from each other. I was working the decoy in the hole. (A wooden, small-fish-looking decoy about seven inches long.) A fish line is attached to its top, metal fin and the other end of the line is attached to an 18-inch stick that you pull up about one foot, and let it "swim" back down in a circle within the hole. The tail fin can be bent so that it swims into whatever size hole that you cut.

We talked for a while, saw a few panfish swim through the hole along the river's bottom. We were fishing in about ten feet of water. Our eyes were becoming glazed over from staring into the water for so long. The dark shack about the hole makes visibility into the water very easy. You can see water bugs swimming most of the time down there.

I'm now, working the decoy, and my wrist is starting to feel like its ready to fall off from the constant jerking motion that you have to do steadily to keep the decoy looking like a real fish. If a northern DOES come after the decoy, it would strike it like a flash of lightning, spit it out and continues on. Most of them though, startle you by just appearing from no where, lay a few feet under the decoy, then slowly come up and try to swallow it whole.

The REAL big one, those in the 8-10 pound class or larger, will glide slowly into the hole at the same depth as the decoy, stop momentarily, size it up, then make a quick dash to claim its supper.

The trick is to continually, watch, watch, watch that hole for a fish sighting. They all normally follow these patterns when they're on the prowl. That, "Moment of pause" is so important because the "decoy operator" must "swim" the decoy in smaller circles and slowly but not to slowly, bring it about a foot from the top of the water. The "man with the spear" Bill, in this case, has a length of rope, as long as the spear itself, attached to the top of the spear and the other end attached to his wrist. For a successful spearing, he must lower the spearhead (it has 5 sharp tines) under the surface of the water so when he decided to heave the spear at the fish, the spearhead doesn't have to break the water's surface and scare away the fish.

Conditions were getting ripe for us to either fall asleep or to see a northern. My eyes, again, were becoming glazed over. Bill looked like he was ready to fall into the hole from such a long time of inaction. We were doing our duty. We were watching that hole intently.
SUDDENLY!!, and I mean SUDDENLY a Huge Northern slid through the hole about two feet below the decoy. We were operating the decoy about three feet below the surface.

That fish looked to be the size around of a good cedar post! He coasted through the hole so slowly that he seemed as long as a good-sized cedar post, and disappeared below the ice outside of the hole's limits. We both tensed up. We knew it was probably the MOTHER OF ALL NORTHERNS. We saw it clearly. To see a fish this huge was an experience, let alone think that we had a chance of spearing one.

We knew it wasn't afraid or shy of us, as we didn't move. I said, "I'll work the decoy up. You set the spear into the water…..real easy. We don't want to miss THIS one!"

I was so intent in working my part of the deal that I wasn't watching Bill. Bill is the only guy in our camp that is prone to get Buck Fever. He can watch a big buck, pull up on it and sometimes forget to shoot.

You're probably ahead of me already with your thinking. Anyway, Bill lowered that spear like the veteran spearer he was. He moved very slowly to take advantage of a position from most every angle to spear in that hole. We waited one, two, five and it seemed like ten minutes. The waiting for the fish to come back is what causes tension and doubt in the spearer's mind. Is that monstrous fish coming back or did we miss our chance by trying to wait for a perfect shot at it?

The quiet, suspense can be deadly on your nerves. SUDDENLY…………without any warning, that monster of a northern reappeared, slowly in our hole. It stopped below us. It was about four feet from the water's surface. It stayed there, working its fins and never taking its eyes off of that decoy.

I said, "Go easy…..and take him, Bill." Bill was rising up slightly from his seat for a well-aimed throw-of-the-spear. Both of us had to be excited. We never saw a northern this large. I quickly estimated that it could run 15-20 pounds. Bill, again, raised the spear handle up about a foot for that good, forceful, jab of the spear.

The fish was intently finning itself, in place, and Bill was poised to throw the spear. NOTHING HAPPENED!!! I looked quickly at Bill and he was "Froze onto the spear." I kept saying in a low voice, "Throw it, throw it….." All of a sudden, he threw the spear about three feet below the surface but wouldn't let go of it!!!

I never saw anything like it. Bill looked like he had high anxiety, a little embarrassed, and the fish swam away….

We just missed the biggest northern that probably lived in that stretch of the Menominee River. We did spear four other smaller northern after that. One was so narrow that it went right between two tines of the spear.

On the trip home, he said, "I don't see any need to tell anyone else about that "miss" that I made with the spear, do you? I was thinking for awhile, then said, "Not if I get to spear for the next four times we go and YOU jiggle that dam decoy…..

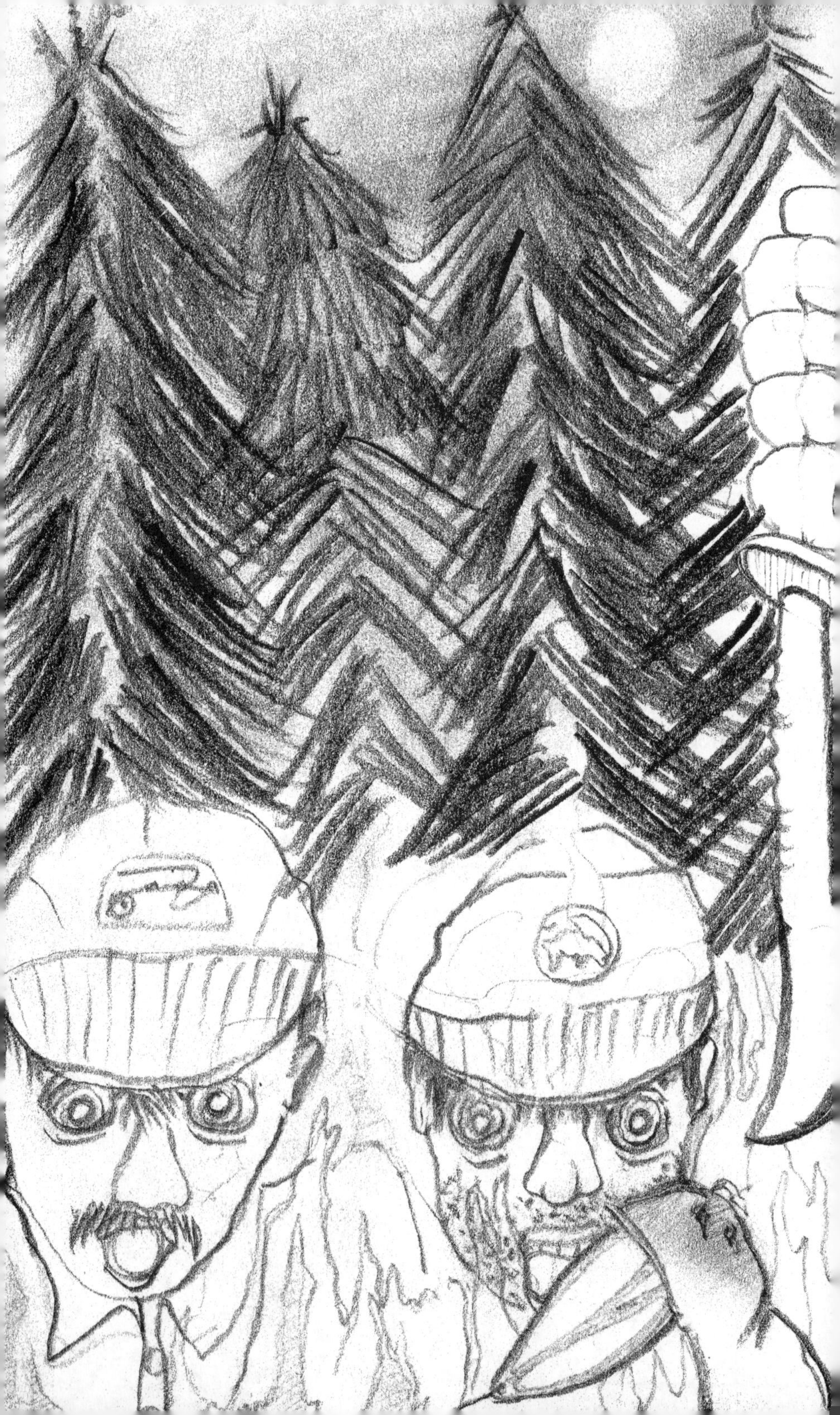

CHAPTER 3

FISHING HAYWARD LAKE

There was no public access to this lake in the 1950's or 60's. Anyone who fished or hunted on it either belonged to the elite Hayward Lake Club or risked their lives sliding a boat over the top of the bog in its half-plugged channel. We were in the latter group.

This was one of the best kept secret lakes for fishing or hunting. It was so easy to get to if you belonged to the "Club". Their buildings were on its one shore. The other shores were old cranberry bog with no bottom if you had the misfortune of breaking through. Breaking through was easy. Sliding your boat down the inlet channel covered with floating bog was a challenge only for the young and hardy. Some might argue, the foolish.

You had to walk alongside of the boat, hang onto it, push the bog down with your weight so the water would run over the top of it. Then, you could slide the boat over it. This had to be done about two feet at a time.

A careful person would break through, at least, 4-5 times and really hang onto the boat so you didn't go under.

The whole process took a full hour to an hour and a half before you'd enter into the lake.

It was not JUST like, but it reminded you of Humphrey Bogart taking the *African Queen* down that passage into the bigger lake.

Once we'd get to the lake, the fishing was always productive. Northerns are still plentiful there. We were casting one day, along the shore and caught a Northern on about every third cast. The "shore" is a floating bog. There are no roots connecting to the lake bottom. The fish hide along the bog and wait for some unsuspecting frog, small duck, or daredevil to swim along its edge. We'd cast, then row the boat along with a pair of copper-tipped oars that I inherited from my Grandfather. As I was rowing, I could feel a bump, bump, onto one of the oars. I watched and as the oar came up for another stroke, a northern was striking at the flashing copper. The copper flashed as it reflected the sun. That's what you call hungry northern.

Another time, three of us were fishing in our 12 foot, flat-bottomed boat out there. The northerns were again, striking the Daredevils about every 3-4 casts.

Dick had a nice one on. He got it in. About a 5 pounder. It just about swallowed the Daredevil. We always carried a long-nosed pliers to take out hooks in northerns. Ever since we met "three-fingers" Ollie, who claims a northern got his fingers, we never took the chance.

Dick took the pliers and hooked it onto his lure and pulled…..it let loose suddenly, and somehow one of the trible hooks ended up way in Dick's thumb. He looked wide-eyed at me for reassurance. It looked bad. It would be no small effort to get that out.

We agreed that we'd go over to the Lake Club and see if they'd drive him to a doctor. This club did not welcome strangers and we were reluctant to go over there.

As we docked, two guys met us by their shore. They were friendly, sympathetic, and also feeling no pain. We told them our problem and one of them started to build a fire. He said that he could fix that. He would cut the hook out. Laying his hunting knife into the fire to sterilize it, he was ready. I thought he was joking. Then, I could see that he was serious. His partner started to back up. Either, not to fall into the fire or else so he wouldn't get any blood on himself.

Dick was turning whiter. He looked as serious as I'm sure he could at me and said, "Don't let them cut me." Being that they were in no shape to drive a car and were confused as to what else they should do, we got into the boat for the "ordeal back through the channel" and to our car.

A quick trip then, into Stephenson, and we found a doctor. Thank God for small-town doctors. This guy looked like he'd take on anything. I quickly looked around. Diplomas on the wall, convincingly looking tools in a cabinet, no blood on the floor, and he calmed us down.

The doctor started mixing some powder with what appeared like water, sucked it up into a needle and gave him a shot in the thumb. I thought, this guy's got everything. We reassured Dick. "Don't worry. This doctor will fix you up with no problems." He looked back at us with eyes like a dog that had his foot caught in a trap for a week. We lived through that one.

Another time, we were going duck hunting on that lake. As big as it is, you could be the only party on it. We never had different, fancy, boats for special occasions. We had that one, flat-bottomed, 12-foot boat that we built ourselves. We used it for river fishing, lake fishing, trapping, fishing on Green Bay when we wanted to live dangerously, and duck hunting.

Well, we put in our penance by working our way through the boggy channel to get into the lake and felt good that we didn't fall in and get wet. Getting wet would have ended the hunt, as the weather was blowing and cold. There were a few snowflakes in the air.

I was in the front of the boat with the shotgun and Jim was rowing us slowly along the shore. Off of the next point of land, we could see about a dozen ducks bobbing in the waves. We squatted down and did our best to inch closer. Finally, I raised up and leveled off on a few. We figured we'd let them fly and we'd have a more killing shot.

Just as it looked like I was going to shoot, a guy jumped up from the shore and said, "Don't shoot, don't shoot! Those are my decoys!" They really did look real. We discovered that the "Club" had a nice floating blind along one side. We eased our boat in under the corn stalks that were wired to the chicken-wire covering.

It was a nice blind, out of the wind. I think that we fell asleep in there for a while. When we woke up, it was snowing and blowing quite heavy. Since we weren't seeing anything to shoot, I stood up to stretch. We figured that we'd get out of there before it got colder. Just as I stood up, a flock of Canadian Geese were coming in (I swear to land in front of this blind.) They looked pretty as a calendar picture, flying low in that blowing snow. They saw me first. They were back-peddling their wings faster than Jim could ever row that boat.

No shots, but a lot of excitement. I always remember that lake for ducks, pine snakes, perch, and big northern. This one June day, we were fishing the lake's shore. I watched a small duck waddle to the shore's edge, jump into the water, and it sat there for about 10 seconds. SUDDENLY, there was a loud splash and a big swirl in the water. The duck completely disappeared. The water, again, became calm. That had to be one big northern. It also gave you a very eerie feeling looking down into that dark, muck-covered, lake bottom.

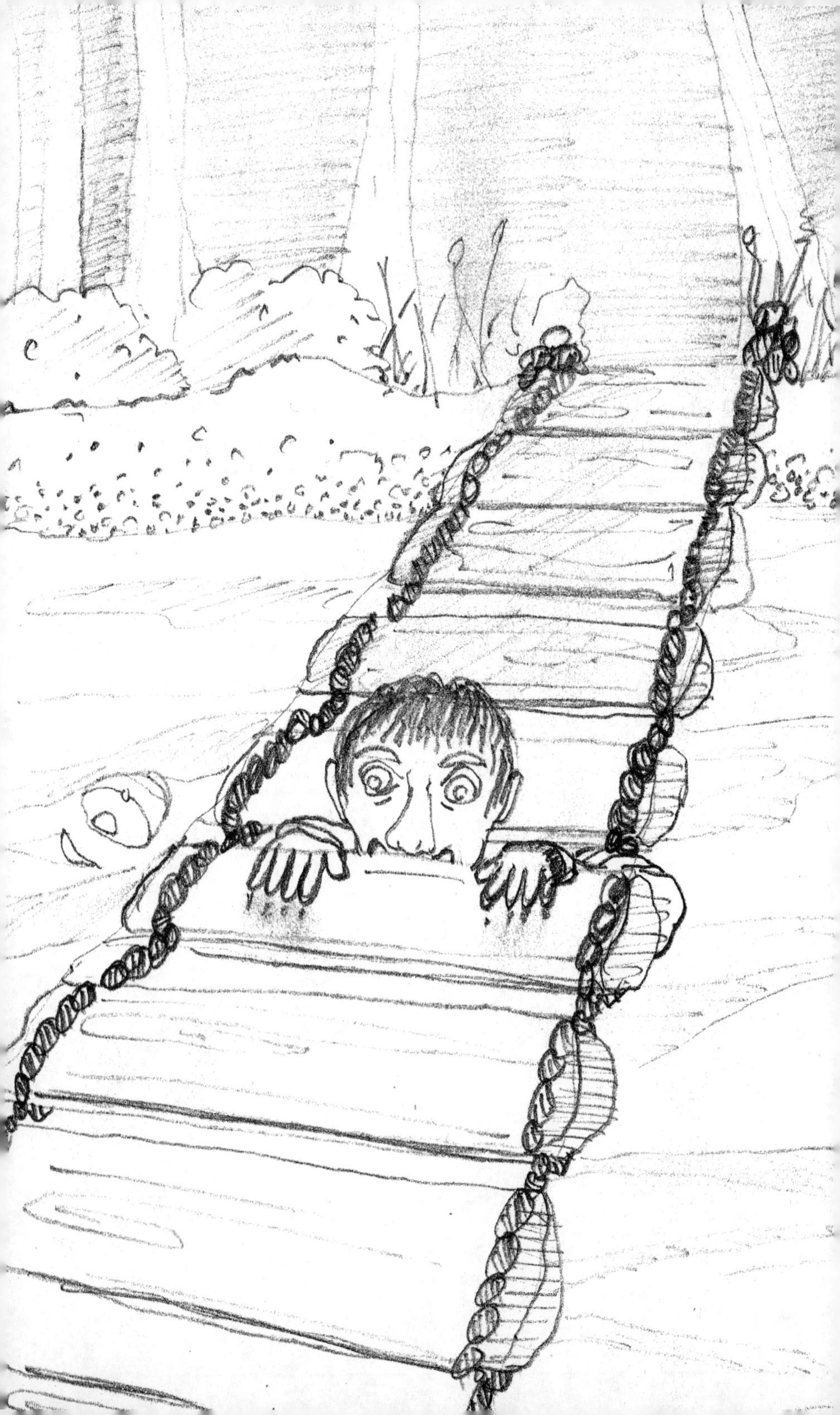

CHAPTER 4

HARD LUCK JOE, THE TROUT FISHERMAN

Joe always seemed to have hard luck. It not only followed him, it seeked him out. I first met him at an insurance fraternal lodge meeting. We were both "picked?" to represent the lodge and vote to represent the members' thinking.

This didn't appear to be a tough job. I sized up the membership that showed up for the meetings and it didn't look like they did too much thinking. I figured a couple of days-paid vacation and bunk with another fisherman. Maybe even, get friendly enough to go fishing together. This was my introduction to Joe.

I drove over to his house to ride with him. His wife came to the door, introduced herself, asked me in and appeared to be a warm, quality person. We were visiting and in came Joe. He was muttering about her not having his shirt ironed like he liked it. "My first wife never would have done this," muttered Joe. His wife physically flinched. I could sense that he pushed the wrong button there. Then I heard a few more, "My first wife this and my first wife that." I was thinking, this guy must like to live dangerously. He didn't say anything nice about his present wife. She in turn, was saying, "Now, Joe…." Or,

"Is that right, Joe?".... but the smile on her face could have killed.

I was starting to get odd feelings about Joe, remembering that I was going to live with him for a few days. Thoughts flashed back to me from the lodge. Some guys said, "Your not really going anywhere with Joe, are you?" "Your not really going to RIDE with him, are you?" They kind of backed away from me like they didn't want to get infected.

Joe was all "doom and gloom" on the way out to the car. "She sure isn't like the first wife…puts the coffee cup on the left side rather than on the right…." Her house was immaculately clean and she appeared very personable. I thought, his first wife must have been a saint!

Joe's car was something else. He had four buttons on the dashboard for shifting. One was low, two, second, three, third, and of course, R was reverse. He started the car, pushed in a button and nothing happened. The button went way into the dashboard and never came out.

"Damn thing!" Joe said, and pushed in another. That one got us going but we were jerking along. I never saw another car like that. Then we were on the highway. He would "tailgate," go to slow, and move over into the other lane. Cars would beep their horns at us as they pulled out of his way. Joe would shout, "Road Hog!" at them. I had my feet pressed into the floor and my shoulders pressed way into the seat. That seat belt didn't seem to be much to hide behind. He seemed to be able to see good enough but it was like driving with Mr. Magoo!

He pulled into the parking lot of the motel, people were jumping out of his way. Joe said, "Never give those pedestrians an inch or they will take all day." I gave them credit for moving so fast, especially that old lady that was almost up against my side window.

We got into our room and he said, "That's another thing she did….got a smokers room. She knows that I don't smoke. Nothing like my first wife…." Then he opened his suit case….. "Damn", he said. "One black sock and one red sock. Now, she HAD to do that on purpose. You can see why I like to go fishing."

I was starting to have second thoughts about wanting to go fishing with him. Normally, everyone likes to go with a different fisherman so you can find a new place to fish. I sat a safe distance away from him and we started to talk fishing. Joe said he liked stream trout fishing and was a good woodsman. He really didn't look like a good woodsman to me but I listened to his stories.

He said, "Last year, I fished with my wife's brother on the Pike River for trout. We were in a canoe. I don't know really what was wrong with him but he was awful jumpy and always kept looking back at me. We were doing well until we went under a log bridge built over the stream. The water's surface level and the bottom of the log bridge didn't allow much clearance. Somehow, when I was passing under there, my head got stuck between two of those bridge logs. It was no joke! I was stuck good!"

"My brother-in-law laughed and laughed as I struggled to pull my head free. It just wouldn't free itself. I thought for a while, and decided, the only way I'm going to get free is to tip the canoe over so I have more clearance.... I tipped the thing over and got free. My brother-in-law looked really mad and wasn't laughing anymore. He lost some fishing gear and said that I should have, at least, told him that I was going to do that. I was thinking, if he wouldn't have been laughing at me so hard, I might have told him. He seemed to be a poor sport. I never did like him anyway. Damn fool!"

I think that Joe caught his share of trout, in his own way, just that hard luck always followed him. Some of the "lodge boys" told me that Joe was fishing out of a friend's camp once. No matter what Joe did, things seemed to go bad for everyone.

He'd put wood in the stove and not shut the lid completely. The place would smoke up before they noticed it. Joe would use the last of the toilet paper in the out-house and forget to tell the next guy to bring a roll out with him.

Joe bragged about the three-pound coffee can that he'd put by his bunk to go to the toilet in, rather than having to go out in the dark night. One night, a couple of the younger guys cut the bottom out of his can. Joe got up in the dark, did his duty, and it streamed onto his blankets and down his leg. They said, "Joe looked up to the sky and said, 'Why is it always me, Lord? Why is it always me?'...."

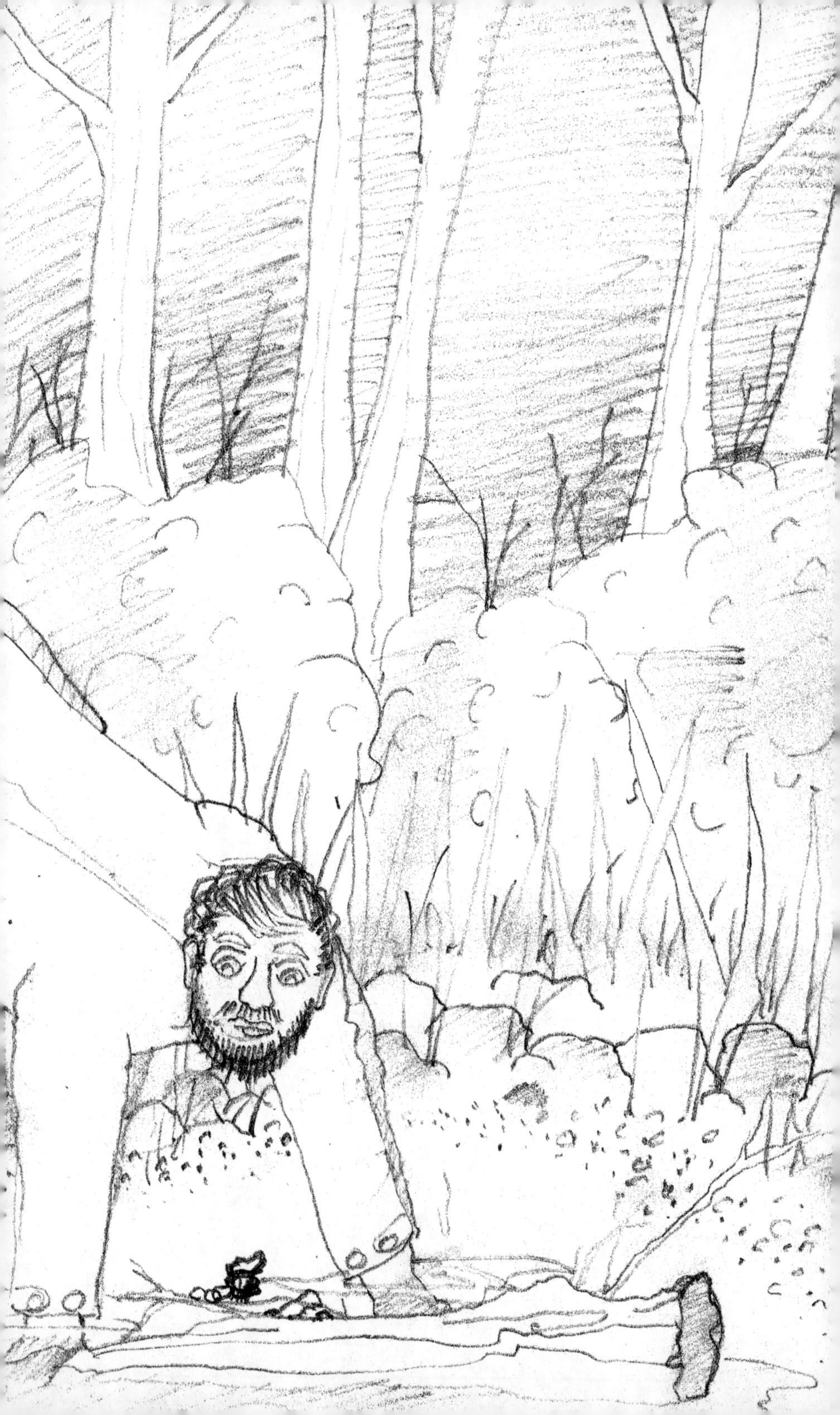

CHAPTER 5

AN UNFORGETTABLE CHARACTER FRANK

He was the best trapper that I have ever known. He told me that he started his trapping career during the Great Depression. It was more a matter of survival than going into it for any sport.

One day, he caught a skunk by his backyard shed. Someone told him that if he had the stomach to skin out its hide, that there was a market for the hides. He could actually get paid money for them.

In no time, he picked up a trap here and a trap there, until he worked up enough for a sizable trap line.

Frank lived along the Menominee River road. He would hang his skunk hides on the clothesline about 40 feet from the road. "After I had 20 or so hides hanging there," he said, "I could notice a distinct drop in neighbors coming over to visit. (You had to be a TRUE friend to stop and visit with that smell.) Even people walking by, walked faster when they got in smelling range of that clothesline. "That's where I learned how to trap and how I got money to feed my family during the depression." "You had to swallow a lot of pride, but in those days, we swallowed a lot of everything."

He was a giant of a man, big, barrel-chested, large features, as his nose, ears, and a VERY loud voice. He later worked as a night watchman in a local paper mill which could have accounted for his shouting when he talked. Anyone that has worked in a paper mill knows it's near impossible to be heard over the roar of those paper machines.

His self-training of skunk trapping helped advance him to trap mink, muskrat, beaver, coon and whatever other furs that had value. He made his own "lures" from the animal musk glands and spent many hours along the river and streams observing the animal habits and best place to set the traps.

After the Depression, he was a well-known area trapper. He would set hundreds of traps. Fur buyers came from as far away as Canada to buy his well-skun-out quality furs.

During the trapping season, he would take two weeks vacation from his watchman job and trap steady, claiming that he made more money trapping, then he could working for the paper mill. His two-stall garage and basement would be hanging solid with mink, coon, beaver, fox, coyote, and muskrat pelts. It was truly a sight to see! No one else would believe that all those fur animals existed if you hadn't seen these results.

He and my Dad were the best of friends. I'd be lucky enough to go with him on his route sometimes. Frank could kick a beaver house and listen for the "ploop-ploop" as beavers would swim out. He'd count how many were there for trapping. Unusual as it may seem, he had the ability to set his beaver traps to catch only the "adult" beavers (these were classified as "blanket" beaver because of their size), and leave the smaller ones to grow and reproduce. He figured, he'd catch them when they were larger and worth more.

There was no game law for this, only common sense by an expert and experienced trapper. You didn't take $10.00 when you could get $75.00 for the same hide after it was fully matured.

His trapping car, that I can remember, was a 1940 "humpbacked" Ford. I believe that his grandson still has this car in good shape, under a canvas in a large metal shed. I saw it a year ago. That probably is his legacy of his grandfather, the trapper. It's still in very good condition.

Frank sometime spend as much time jacking that car up, putting logs under it to free it from spring mud holes in back roads that no one else would attempt to drive on. These were the places, though, where the beavers were active. It was always at spring high water, flood time.

Frank was also an accomplished, Brook Trout, fly fisherman. Many of these beaver ponds that he trapped were also prime holders of trophy brook trout. He was usually the first one or one of the first to find these spots because of his persistent drive to walk many miles to trap the beaver. Being a practical man, he'd prefer flies to fish but would also use worms. Whatever they would bite on.

He had a homemade, tin-lined, "worm bed" to reproduce and hold his worms when it would be hard to dig them in the dry season. One day, I was over to his place and he was "balling out" his son because his grandson was taking all of his worms and, of course, not digging any to put back. His son promptly turned to his boy and said, "Damn it. I told you not to go into Grandpa's worm bed when he's home. Wait till he goes to town or work before you go in there." Frank looked at him and just rolled his eyes. He never seriously got mad at anyone but you could imagine what he was thinking.

To watch him work his fly-rod on a trout river or pond was a sight to behold. Many times, I would reel in my line and just watch the artistic rhythm he's set up with laying that fish line just where he wanted it. He always caught the big ones. They must have responded to that fly first and it always seemed like such a natural bait on the water when he'd lay it down.

I mentioned before, that Frank had a roar as loud as someone shouting when he'd talk. He had a heart just as big. On these fishing trips, he'd pack a huge lunch for himself and Dad, my brother and I had our lunch bag. As he was driving and about ½ of the way to the Pike River, he'd lean toward the back seat and tell us kids, "Take whatever sandwiches you want out of my bag, just leave something for me to eat too." We'd eat his "extra thick" ham sandwiches and leave him our "egg salad" sandwiches. At lunch time, he'd say, "This is the first time I ate these egg sandwiches since our last fishing trip."

Frank's land bordered the Menominee River and was about 10 miles out of the City of Menominee. In the spring, he'd pull "deadheads" (logs from the historic logging days on the Menominee River that would be showing one end above the water's surface and the other stuck into the river bottom). He built a raft with a four-foot square hole in the middle with a box-like frame around it rising about waist-high. It had the appearance of a "wishing well." Above this, he had a handmade wench with a strong rope wound around it connected to iron "logging tongs."

He'd spot a "deadhead" log bobbing its one end above the waterline, float his raft over it, clamp on the iron logging tongs and crank the wench until the raft would go about a foot below the water's surface. The pressure created would work the stuck end free from the river's bottom. Somehow, he managed to pull the log up and pile them onto the shore.

After allowing them to dry, he'd later cut them into one-inch boards, 2 by 4's, and 2 by 6's for building. My present cabin's front room walls are all finished inside with these rough-cut, "deadhead" boards bought from him. They are a distinct remembrance of the early "logging days" in Menominee's history. We call it "Frank's room" in honor of him.

Frank was a natural storyteller. WHATEVER story he told, seemed to keep you spellbound. One that I remember well was, we were riding to a particular trout river and Frank started to tell us about two mink that he saw mating. He said, "The male was holding the back of the female's neck with his teeth and he was mating for all he was worth." Dad getting red, uncomfortable, and cringing in his seat as Frank was going into more detail. We kids (brother and I) were listening and hoping for MORE detail. He said to my dad, "It's O.K. You've got to explain this sexual stuff to them sooner or later." It was a little BEFORE our time or needs, so we were learning something special.

I can remember my Dad's reaction. He said, "I don't think either one of them is ever going to mate with a mink." Frank then roared with laughter and the whole car shook from side to side. He did arouse our curiosity but we weren't really sure, what for? We felt that we had some valuable information but didn't know what to do with it. Like a dog barking at a moving car tire. If the car stopped, the dog would look puzzled and just walk away.

On the last roads of the trout trips, he'd drive through dirt roads and parts of tall grass fields if he could find one. Then when we stopped, we'd pick the grasshoppers caught in the car radiator to use for fish bait.

Frank was a legend in his own time. Some trappers would be very mad at him if he moved slightly into their territory. They knew he could catch furs that would outsmart their trap sets. I often thought it was interesting how each "established" trapper seemed to have their territory to trap. There were no boundaries other than each one honoring the other's turf.

He died from a heart attack while checking traps in a very remote area in Menominee County. His son was with him. As Frank was such a huge man, there was no way his son could have carried him out of the woods and he didn't want to leave him there alone while he went for any help. His son made a 3-log raft, laid Frank on it and floated him a mile downstream to where their car was parked.

Had Frank known about his ride downstream, he'd have liked that. He loved the woods and the streams.

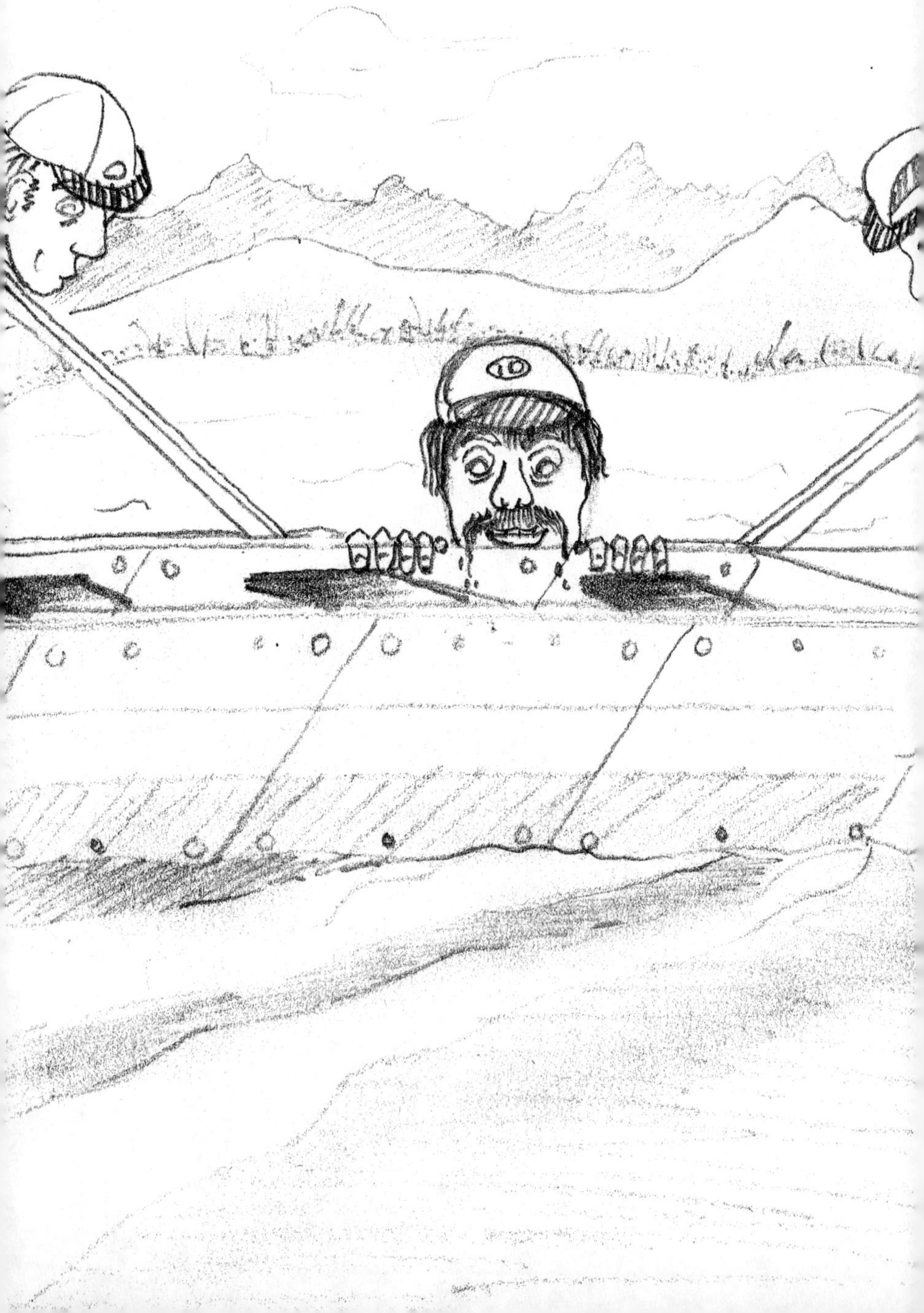

CHAPTER 6

GRANDPA FRED AND THE PLYWOOD BOAT

I made that plywood boat. It fit two people very comfortably with all the extra fishing gear, landing net, anchor, gas can, and extra clothes, just right. We normally fished with THREE people on each fishing trip. Someone extra always seemed to want to go along.

On this one, particular trip, there was my brother, Bill, my 82 year old Grandfather, and myself. Because of the boat's size, (it was 12 feet long) everything had to "just fit" and there wasn't any "wiggling around" room. This homemade boat had no gunnels like an aluminum boat has to help stabilize it and to hold it up higher in the water if you had an extra-heavy load. Its sides were straight plywood. Each overweight pound made it sink noticeably lower into the water. (Picture yourself taking a floating coffee cup in the kitchen sink full of water and pressing (forcing) the cup down lower in the water than its natural level.)

We'd kind of wiggle our bottoms on the seats while we were still close to the shore to test our ability to keep afloat. If it looked O.K., we'd pass the danger out of our minds and go fish, real scientific.

We were going out this time, early in the morning on the first week of June. That's the best time to fish spawning panfish over their spawning beds on Shakey Lakes. We use either a two-joint bamboo pole or a fly rod with a small popper. The bamboo poles make it easy to swing out a pole's length (about 8 feet plus the pole's length) of line right on top of a nice, white, spawning bed. A light bobber and a hook with a worm are also an excellent set-up.

The water is still very clean in this chain of five lakes. Whoever sits in the front of the boat watches for spawning beds along the shore in about two feet of water. Then, we shut off the motor, hold our position farther off-shore, and throw the lines over the spawning beds. Usually, if you see one bed, there are many more so there is a lot of action.

The bobber will dip down about a ½ inch if one is biting and then, it starts moving to one side for about a three-foot run. It's a matter of setting the hook and you have a scrappy Bluegill on the line.

This day, the spawning beds were plentiful. If we'd find one, there seemed to be nine more all together. The biggest and tastiest panfish always bite during the spawning season. This was an excellent sport for my 82-year-old Grandfather who loved fishing but couldn't, of course, walk the trout stream shores anymore. His eyesight was not the best but he never complained and loved to be out fishing.
We'd tell him about where the spawning bed was and he'd throw his line in the general direction. We'd tell him when to pull and he'd set the hook on some nice ones, the same as we would. All was going well. The

fish were biting unbelievably well. This was THE day to be fishing! Whatever it was, they were biting fast and furious.

We'd move to new spawning beds as we caught out the big ones. The nice thing about these lakes, the water is so clear that you can move your popper or worm away from the small ones and play for the big ones.

As we were moving slowly, a big loon flew off of its nest on a deserted beaver house. If it wouldn't have moved, we never would have seen the nest. We checked it out. There were two nice sized eggs, so, you could expect two new loons to hatch. Then, you just had to say, "Good luck" to them.

Where this old beaver house is located, is some of the deepest water in the lake. The lake is noted for some monster Northern Pike. I hooked onto one last year that was about four feet long. As I was using a spinning rod at the time, chances of tiring it out and getting it were good. He fought for what seemed 10 minutes. Then, it slowly, seemingly, like he didn't even have a fish lure in his mouth. I put my big landing net with the two-foot long handle down into the water to net him, headfirst like a real pro.

I pulled up on the aluminum net and its bottom and one side was missing. That fish was gone in a flash. He fought his way right out of that nylon netting. I wondered how long he kept that daredevil before it disintegrated from his stomach acids.

Anyway, in that same location another year, I saw a mother duck and three little newborns swimming in a line behind her. All at once, there was a swirl in the water by the last one and it disappeared. We motored closer and saw a huge Northern cruising near the surface. That thing looked scary enough that I was glad I was in the boat.

Back to fishing with Gramps. This day, we were catching such nice ones that we hated to quit. Grandpa said, "Take me to the shore, I have to go to the toilet." Brother Bill said, "Try to hold it awhile. We just got set over these new spawning beds." About 10 minutes later, Grandpa said, "Take me to the shore. I have to go bad." We just sat there, enthused with the fishing that we kind of had him tuned out.

A few minutes later, there was a big splash on the side of the boat and the boat rocked up higher in the water! The spray got us all wet. I grabbed on to a side to prevent falling out and looked behind me ………. Grandpa was gone!

As quickly as THAT happened, he bobbed back up and grabbed onto the side of the boat. There he was. All wet with his white mustache drooping down from all of the water. After a moment, we figured out that he took it upon himself to stand up and relieve himself over the side, lost his balance, and fell in……..

We didn't know if we should feel bad or laugh. I know if that would have been my Dad rather than Grandpa, he'd have been thinking about choking whoever he could reach first!! Grandpa looked at us as surprised as we looked at him. Then he smiled. He was in about four feet of water as the fish spawning beds are always close to the shore. He stood up, and said, "Now, I think we better go in so I can change clothes." He seemed as embarrassed as we thought it was funny.

After all, he was the greatest hunter and fisherman that we had known. He was always a quiet-natured person.

When my brother and I were younger and Grandpa was still driving, he'd come over and pick us up to go stream trout fishing with him. He had a 1934 Chev sedan, four-door. It seemed, if you sat in the back seat, your legs would hang down like sitting on a kitchen chair. It also seemed that you could take a step and one-half before you reached the back of the front seat. His eyesight had to be a long way from 20/20 vision anymore. On the way home, he'd be driving down highway 41, go off with two wheels on the gravel, (the right side of the car would drop down six inches from running off of the paved road), he'd get back onto the road and the car would level off again.

When this would happen, he'd say, "Did I scare you, boys?" SCARE us? No one had a scarier ride than that at a carnival. He always stayed near the road's shoulder though and never went near the centerline. Later, either he scared himself driving (although, it didn't seem like anything could scare him) or he thought enough was enough because he gave that old car to my brother and I.

He put it up on blocks "Until we were old enough to drive it." Before we got to use it, somehow, the radiator cap came off and squirrels put some corn kernels in that radiator. We'd fill the radiator full of water and carry a few gallons of extra water in that huge back seat. After about 10-20 miles, the radiator would start boiling over. The white steam coming out of that radiator as we were driving along reminded you of an old steam train coming down the road.

We'd watch the water gauge on the dashboard. When it registered "FULL HOT", we'd stop, fill it up again and drive on, always with one eye looking for another creek to get water.

After his eyes got progressively worse, he'd make excuses why he couldn't go fishing with us. We'd then, borrow his hip boots for each trip. He had the best hip boots that I ever saw. He still liked to periodically, go out in that plywood boat to fish. We'd tell him about where the panfish were, he'd throw in his worm and was as successful as if he did the whole thing himself.

He gave us a pair of boat oars that had a neat layer of copper metal nailed onto the ends for protection from rocks, etc. We used these until I finally sold the boat and bought my first aluminum 14-footer.

The new boat was safer and had much more room. Somehow, it lacked the thrill and character of that old plywood boat.

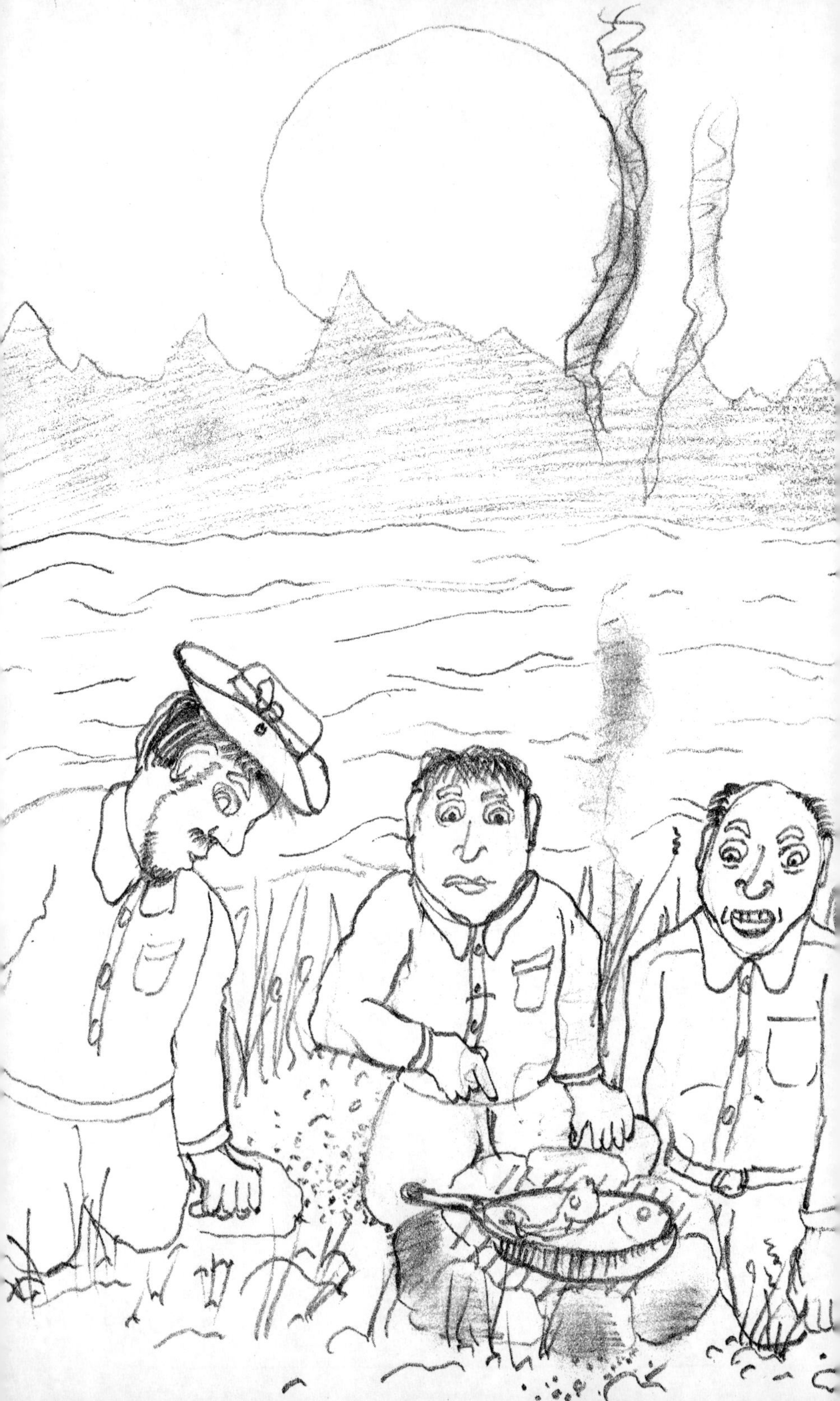

CHAPTER 7

A WILD FISHING ADVENTURE
(WITH A FINNISH TOUCH)

We started to plan this trip about a year ago. Our party of 4 (four always fit into the fly-in planes just right), Don from Stephenson, Bob from Daggett, Dave from Marinette, and the other Bob from Gillett.

This year's trip was planned to a new lake for us, about a hour's drive Northwest of Thunder Bay, Ontario. We were going for perch and walleye. We heard stories of catching perch by the 100's and taking home your Coleman cooler full of fillets. Who wouldn't want to do that? The more guys that we talked to, the better it sounded.

We were primed and ready to go. Even seasoned fishermen like us were buying a few new lures, "just in case." A week before the trip, Dave called that he had an emergency triple bi-pass surgery and couldn't make the trip. Disappointedly, he said, "But be sure to put me down for next year." We got Vic, from Oconto Falls, to come out of fishing retirement to replace Dave for the trip.

On July 25th, we started North in two pick-up trucks. Don came up with 2, two-way transmitters to use between the trucks for communication. I thought, Wah, we were in "high cotton" this year. Going to a cabin with hot water, shower, and bedrooms rather than our normal fly-in that has a one-room cabin, bunks, outdoor "one-holer," and where running water means one of our guys runs to the lake to fill a pail. This new cabin was laid out a lot like our U.P. deer camps.

We drove for 13 hours, saw one moose and one black bear in Canada.

The cabin owner furnished the boats, motor, and gas. The 7-day cabin, boat, motor, and gas were cheaper than our fly-in trips for 4 days out of WaWa.

It was 95°F the morning we left. Our night crawlers "fried" on the way up. Even a self-respecting robin wouldn't have bit one of those. We got fresher ones just outside of Superior, WI. On the way up, the excitement was building and we wondered if we took enough coolers to take all of those 100's of perch we planned to catch (perch are considered a 'rough fish' in Canada and there is no bag limit).

We arrived with daylight to spare. The cabin was even more than what we expected. The owners, Rick and Norma, kept them exceptionally clean. The first day on the water, the perch were biting very little and the walleye even less. It was 95°F there at this time.

The second day, we invited the owners, Rick and Norma to eat with us. They were exceptionally nice people and would do whatever they could to make you "happy campers." Rick sensing that we weren't to happy with what we caught so for, asked me if we'd be interested in hiring a guide to go to a remote, smaller lake for walleye.

He said, "The guide is Finnish, is very good at his work, reasonably priced and likes a little booze." He also said, "If you decide to hire him, go easy on the booze or he may not show up the next day."

The guys were pretty low on the fishing already. Don said, "Vic was singing, 'The squaws along the Yukon are good enough for me,' for about the 100th time. I swore, if he sang that song once more, I was going to tip over the boat."

Everyone wanted to take the guide. Rick called him for us that night and way late, he came to see us. His name was Auntti Romu (pronounced, Aunt=but like the English pronunciation of Aunt…… a short A sound……….then, tee. AAAuntee, or Auntii. He talked ½ Finnish and looked like he just came off the Lewis and Clark expedition……a real woodsman.

Auntii was a story by himself. He was about 5' 11", white mustache, walked with a "pumping" motion (like he was stepping over logs). He wore a checkered shirt, 12" boots laced ½ way up, an Australian hat with the wide rim turned up on one side and chin strap secured under his chin…..and he was smiling. He seemed forever happy. Nothing on the whole trip was negative to him.

He looked like he could wrestle a bear, sleep outside without a blanket, or survive "in the bush" with a knife and a fish hook.

He arrived at our cabin that night in an old pick-up that groaned like it was happy to be riding on a flat road, for a change. He jumped out of his truck. It was a VERY high pick-up without running boards or any step. The first thing you noticed about him was his smile and the twinkle in his eyes.

We all sat down around a long table in the cabin and poured out a generous (like a double shot) for Auntii and single ones for us.

He liked that. His eyes seemed to glow under his bush-white eyebrows. He started to unwind the detail about a "secret" lake full of walleye that he would take us to. He said it had huge northern in it also if we wanted them.

We all had another round of drinks. Auntii's description of those fish seemed to be getting bigger. He started to talk quicker and with a "clipped-off sound after most of his words." He was on a roll and was even getting HIMSELF excited! "There are BIG walleye in der." "GOD DAMN BIG WALLEYE!!" "Pardon my language but I get excited. Some are so big, I scare myself."

Then one of the guys pulled the bottle more to the middle of the table. Auntii kind of raised up in his chair, smiled, and said, "Don't put it too far away." We gave him another one. He downed it and his eyes started to dance all around. He was telling stories, telling us what to bring for bait and "bring bait in a small-pocket sized container." "I want no 'tool boxes' in our small boats (referring to city folk's huge tackle boxes). Auntii licked his lips when I put a few ice cubes in his drink. He said, "Careful, don't splash and spill any. Now, I'll tell you what to bring with. Bring sunglasses, life jackets, landing nets (big ones), sandwiches, jig baits with pink heads and white bodies, and a camera. Don't forget to take pictures of the fish and myself because I like to get my picture took."

Auntii looked out the window at the huge lake that we were by and all of the boats out there and many more tied to the docks. He said, "It will be about a 2 hour drive from this aluminum city (referring to all of the aluminum boats around us), I'll pick you up at 11:00 a.m. tomorrow and we'll get back here at 11:00 p.m." Vic said, "No, no, let's leave at 8:00 a.m. and get home before it gets dark. I don't like to be out there after dark."

Auntii smiled and said, "O.K. When you have your fill of a beautiful shore lunch and a limit to take home, you will want to quit early anyway." With that, Auntii shook hands and said he'd see us early the next day. He said, "You know, you can't guarantee fish to bite. I'm excited. You should catch many, many fish tomorrow."

He got in his truck, it snorted like it was getting ready to climb a big hill. He seemed to be laughing to himself alone in his truck....and then he was gone.

After he left, we were all excited. Were his stories true? Vic said, "I think we gave him too much booze and he'll sleep in tomorrow." Don said, "He probable will come but be way late." I bet Don a dollar that Auntii would show and actually be early. Don looked skeptical but wouldn't take the bet. None of us are high rollers in betting and he must have thought that I saw something that he didn't see.

Bob, our newest fishing partner, from Daggett, said, "If he can show us fish, I'll catch them."

The next day, Auntti arrived 5 minutes early. He bounced out of that high truck like someone on springs. You'd swear that he slept 24 hours, showered, kissed his best girl and was READY. "Come on boys", he said, "The weather's just right and the fish are waiting. I can't wait to taste that beautiful shore lunch" (he was doing the cooking).

We went down a main road, a secondary road, then we went down another secondary road and into a "road under construction area". I told Auntti that in the States, we have good looking "flag girls" on each end, so the drivers don't get so mad waiting to go through." He said, "We have flag girls too but they wouldn't win any prizes. Some drivers swear at them and give them the finger. You have to be careful, if you don't drive like they want, they'll chase you with their sign and swing it at your car."

The next road was a logging truck road. The logging trucks were coming down it at an unbelievable speed. They raised so much dust that you had to stop for a while to re-find the road. They also seemed to be aiming at us as they passed on THEIR narrow road. Then we turned off to the last road. I was riding with Auntti in his truck and Don was following in his "spanking new" 1999, ½ ton Ford with our other two guys, Vic and Bob.

I'll tell you, when I saw the next road, boulders as big around as a Webber grill, little gravel between them, up-hill, down-hill, no sides on the road except the road itself,

I never in my wildest dreams thought that we'd drive on it. I thought that this is where we begin the portage.

Not so, Auntti kept talking just like he was driving downtown. He drove very slowly. It seemed like each front wheel was reaching out and feeling for a top of a rock to drive on. We moved slowly to the next rock and it would repeat itself.

My rear end was bouncing up and down about 6 inches off the seat as we drove. Then, he seemed to have one side down for a while and the door side up, as my bottom was bouncing flat against my door and I was hanging onto whatever would hold. The glove case flew open, a pill bottle jumped out along with some loose papers. They were rolling all over the floor.

Auntti smiled and said, "It's not so bad when you got the steering wheel to hold onto. He didn't seem to be doing much steering as the front wheel banging onto the rocks seemed to set the direction.

Then we stopped once about ¾ of the way through this road as we were in a deep hole. Auntti wanted to stop so the other truck noticed this hole. My feet were against the dashboard and I was hanging onto the back of the seat.

Auntti said, "If your partner can make it through that hole, we won't have to worry about him." I was thinking, at least Don's still got that baby under warrantee (it was only about four months old). Auntti was smiling and the Lord must have been smiling as both trucks bounced to the end of that road.

When I got out of the truck, I looked at my three partners in the other truck. None were talking. Even Vic was not talking. They looked like someone took a shot at them and missed them by an inch.

Auntti bounced out of the truck smiling and said, "Here's where we start to port-tugee. Look at that beautiful lake (you could see parts of it through the woods, about 40 acres away). We are going to catch lots of fish."

He had two motors, a four-horse and a six-horsepower. Of course, the six-horse was a heavier and bigger motor. He said, "One of you will have to carry the six-horse as I had triple bi-pass last year and I am not supposed to carry two motors like I normally do." He opened his shirt and showed us the scars.

We all agreed that Bob, from Daggett, was in the best physical shape for that. The three of us were all shaking our heads, "A-hun, that's right Bob, you can do it." Bob looked back, skeptical but willing. The rest of us were looking serious and grateful. Auntti threw the four-horse on his shoulder, filled his other arm with shore lunch equipment and stepped off like a soldier on the march.

Bob pulled that six-horse up waist high, gritted his teeth and was second. The rest of us took everything else except the spare tire and followed along. At this point, we were shy one gas can because it tipped over on that last road.

We reached the lake after taking only one rest break. Auntti took two "boat plugs" out of his pocket and began screwing them into the boats. They weren't commercial types that you see in the "bailing hole" of the boat, but were two pipe plugs, like a plumber would place, into the end of a pipe to plug the water flow. He said that he has to take the plugs with him so no one uses his boats. I couldn't imagine anyone else coming down that road.

We started fishing. The lake is back-woods Canada solitude. The shoreline was untouched by the ax or any human sign. We're thinking, this was worth the whole trip. Auntti and I were in one boat and Vic, Bob, and Don were in the other. Don and Bob are quiet and serious fishermen. Vic is a real talker and Ya,……. probably enjoys talking more than fishing. As they passed us on one side, I could hear Vic say, "Did you hear the one about "Wood-eye?".... a joke. A half-hour later, they passed us again and hollered, "Do you have any duct tape? We want to use it on Vic so he don't talk so much." Vic got the idea for awhile, and fished quietly. Thereafter, when he started talking too much, someone would say, "Where's the duct tape?" and he'd quiet down. The rest of us snored so I suppose he felt he didn't have the only vice.

We saw eagles on the lake. Up close and sitting in the trees. We caught 6 walleye and two good.sized northern for our shore lunch. I'll say this for Auntti, he handled all the shore lunch chores and cooked up a mouth watering mess of fish. He boned them all and had his own blend of fish breading with Cajun spicing. Just a touch.

It tasted as good as any choice steak. There must have been 6-8 pounds of fish, beans, bread, cookies, beer, and pop. We ate it all. We picked blueberries by the handfuls when Auntti was frying up the meal. They were ripe and plentiful.

"Daggett Bob" fished off of a huge boulder when the meal was being made. He caught a northern in the 10-20 pounds size but lost it trying to ease it up onto the rock.

After a short rest, we loaded up the boats again, shoved off of the island, and began fishing. Everyone caught fish and took home a limit of walleye. It was late afternoon and was beginning to cloud up quickly. The lake was bigger than we thought at the first look. The shoreline all looked alike. There was a beer can hanging on a limb of a tree where we portaged in. I don't know if Auntti looked for it or if he could smell it. Whatever, he found it where we didn't even notice it to find our direction.

The sun was starting to go down when we hit the shore. I looked back and saw an eagle soaring low across the lake. He seemed to be able to glide for a ½ mile without moving his wings. What a beautiful sight! We loaded up and Auntti said, "Der's that gas I said I had, boys. It's all over the back of the pick-up."

We then eased the trucks out again, over those roads (probably made for moose travel only) and reached a main, secondary road. There, we encountered logging trucks. The phrase "Eat my dirt" could have come from these roads. The trucks were huge, loaded with "telephone pole" length logs. The drivers seemed to drive as fast as they could and enjoyed aiming at pick-ups as they would speed by.

Auntti was driving our lead truck. He'd pull over fast at the last minute and shout something in Finnish at them that didn't sound too nice. Then we'd all cough from the cloud of dust. Auntti smiled and said, "A beer will sure go good after this dust." Labatts Blue, Canada's best. I told my old wife, if I ever need blood, tell them to pour in some Labatts instead."

On the way back, he told me that he is a professional trapper, leases a trapping territory from the Province, is a bear and moose guide, fishing guide, and a fun-lovin' Fin, with a smile.

He said that he was at a fur rendezvous last year and had some furs displayed to sell. A lady came up to him and commenced to "take him down" for animal cruelty in trapping those furs. He said, "I told her, 'Lady, I didn't harm those animals. The mountain lion there was a road kill that I skun out, the timber wolf hide was given to me in exchange for some work I did. So I didn't trap them. But that black bear skin, there, now that's where you got me. I just shot it for the hell of it. One day, my old woman was hanging out clothes and that bear started to attack her. I don't know why, but I did shoot it just for the hell's of it.' The lady looked at me, didn't say anymore and left me alone."

Auntti said he was thinking of placing an ad in the *Thunder Bay* newspaper to take a troubled teenage boy for a month to make a mountain man out of him as much as he could in a month. He could hunt, trap, fish, and be in the woods with me. I asked him what he'd do if the kid out-right refused to obey and respect him. He said that he'd probably have to send him back home but, "I'd keep the money though."

We rode alone getting closer to our cabin. I was hoping that he'd take a longer way back as his stories, good humor, and fishing tips were really interesting.

He said, "Who was the guy talking and singing in the other boat all the time?" I said that was Vic. He thought for a while and said, "I didn't mind, as long as he pours those good drinks." Then he sang, "Blue, blue, blue is the sky……….. and also blue is the Labatts, HA HA. Just think, I meet nice, new friends, go fishing, and even get paid for this."

He showed me a picture of himself from last year when he had long white hair and a bushy white beard. "I went to Duluth in December and applied for one of those Santy Claus jobs." With a smile, he said, "They never called me back so I figured those Yankees didn't have any kids that could understand a Finnish Santa."

We caught fish on the main lake after that but everything was anti-climatic after Auntti" fishing with us, and he said, "Watching over you like a mudder hen."

Back at our cabin, we stayed up to 11:45 p.m. one night telling stories, 12:15 p.m. the next night, and 1:30 a.m. the following night. We felt that relationships were more important than fish. That's what we call "camp life" back home in the U.P. hunting camps. We didn't even get around to talking "100%" about girls, which is normal for most healthy fishermen. We did plot a little about chipping in and fixing Vic up with someone from the Thunder Bay Escort Service though. After all, we felt anyone who tells the same jokes twice, deserved something special too.

We traveled a total of 1,052 miles. Our last stop before home was at Hearsh's Supper Club, just down the highway from Iron Mountain, for, as Auntti would put it, "A beautiful buffet!!!" Was it worth it? The sounds of the lake loons in the evening, the quiet nights, fishing, adventures with Auntti, the friendships in sharing stories……….. it won't be long and we'll be planning something for next year.

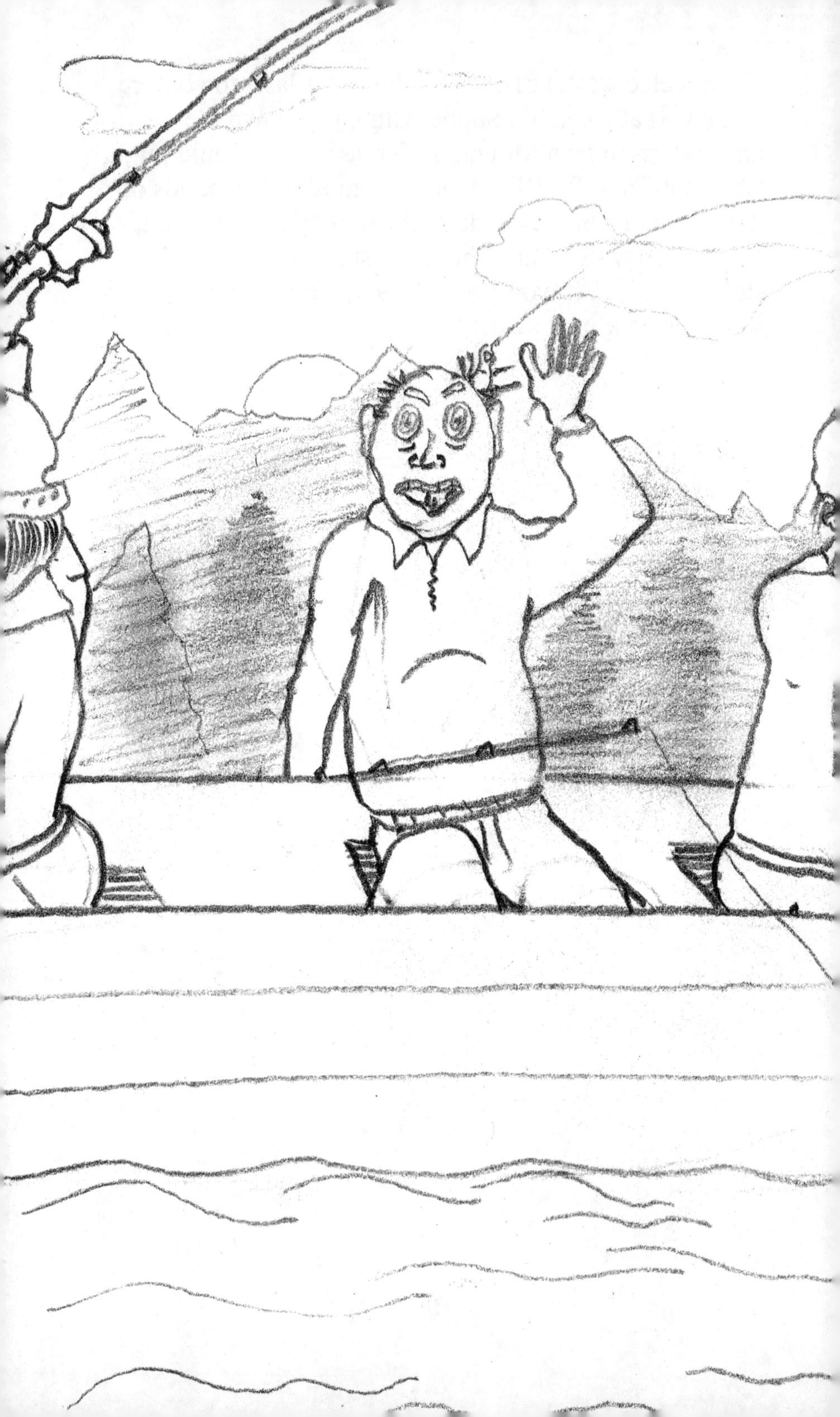

CHAPTER 8

BASS FISHING AMONG THE DEADHEADS

The Big Cedar River, flowing past the town of Cedar River, was one of the best black bass fishing areas in the U.P.

There was a lot of "deadheads" (logs with one end floating above the water and the other stuck into the muddy river bottom). These were left over from the historical logging days.

Whenever there was a "deadhead" bobbing in the water, there normally were a few bass under it. Two fishing buddies of mine and I planned on taking my flat-bottomed, plywood boat up there for the opening day of bass season.

As we were loading our gear to go, John's Dad came out of their house and asked if we'd take him along. Now, anyone who fished out of a 12-foot boat, especially a flat-bottomed plywood one, knows that three in the boat touches on dangerous. It would ride low in the water. Four in that boat would be like putting five gallons of water in a four-gallon pail.

He said that he'd fish from the shore so there'd be no problem with the boat. So, four of us were bouncing up M-35 to Cedar River at 6:00 a.m. on the Saturday of the Opener.... There were always a lot of boats up there for Opening Day. We wanted to get in on some of the "first" fishing of the day.

We arrived, started to put all of the gear in the boat and the motor on. I was always skeptical of how far down the sides of the boat would go from all of this weight. There were no stabilizers (roll guard) built into the side of this boat like a v-bottomed aluminum one has.

We were set to go. Joe found a spot on the riverbank and seemed content fishing there. We were all fishing with worms and a heavy, lead sinker. The heavy sinker did two things. It got your hook to the bottom quickly and also made it possible for you to cast an extra 20-30 feet.

We started to catch some nice bass from the boat. Our three-horse power motor would move us slowly to another "deadhead" and our luck would start all over again. Joe was watching us, intently, from the shore. It looked like he was having a personal war with the mosquitoes.

They were plentiful on the shore, but none out in the breeze where we were. "How about letting me fish in the boat for awhile?" Joe said. "I'll switch with someone." We looked at him fighting those mosquitoes and Bill felt sorry for him. "I'll take a walk down the road for a ½ hour and Joe can take my place."
Bill was always good-natured and must have felt sorry for him sitting with those mosquitoes. His son, John, and

I felt sorry for him too, but not quite that bad that we were going to give up our seats.

We made the exchange and Joe had the middle seat. He was a good fisherman, so I felt satisfied that he wouldn't do any "foolish" moves in the boat. Bill disappeared down the road somewhere. As long as you kept moving, the mosquitoes weren't too bad on the shore.

We were still catching an occasional bass but not as quickly as when we started. I mentioned that Joe was a good fisherman. He also was a lucky fisherman. He'd fish on one side of the boat and his son, John, fished on the other. Joe would get a bite, a second bite, and John wasn't getting anything. All at once, John reeled in and threw in on Joe's side. He fished about a foot away from Joe's line.

Joe looked at him, disgusted, reeled in, and threw in on the other side. He immediately got bites on that side. John, then, reeled in and threw his heavy sinker in by Joe's. Joe then, moved back onto the other side and again, got bites. This went on for a good length of time. Finally, on one "cross-over", John hit Joe square in the head with his 2-ounce sinker. Joe said, "That's it, That's it! Take me to the shore!" He went up to the car and slept until we were done fishing.

We each got a limit of bass and decided that we'd come back the next day. Joe thanked us, without smiling, when we got home. He said that he had something else to do tomorrow. It must have been something REAL important, as Joe had a passion for fishing. When we left him, he was rubbing his head.

The next day, we planned on going back for late afternoon and do some evening fishing with bass lures. That three horsepower motor trolled down to a crawl. You could feel the action of the lures as they moved through the water.

We picked up some bass, but not as many as we got on the first day. Trolling with three fish lines behind a small boat takes some skill. Two poles have to point straight out on each side. The person running the motor fishes straight off the back of the boat.

This all works well until you make a big turn with the boat. Everyone must watch their line carefully so they don't tangle with each other.

Then, it got dark. We ran into another problem. Trolling became too difficult with the three lines after dark, as you couldn't see them to keep them separate. We then would cast, reel in, and hope to pick up a bass this way.

It was really dark. You couldn't tell when one was casting or another was getting ready to cast. So, we came up with a system. The person in the front of the boat was "one." The person in the middle of the boat was "two." The back person was "three."

We agreed that number one would shout, "one," and the other two wouldn't cast. Then, number two would shout, "two," and it would be his turn to cast, and so on……
This worked well until someone got impatient and started casting too soon. In no time, the lines were all tangled up overhead.

We quit before someone ended up with a fish lure stuck in him. That was really a prime spot for fishing. Catching a lot of bass there, seeing Joe get hit in the head with that heavy sinker, and John switching sides so much, were the big memories from that trip.

CHAPTER 9

TWO UNFORGETTABLE CHARACTERS WILLIE & BILLY

These two guys were bachelor brothers. I never did get a good explanation why they were named so close together. Their father's name was William. Their mother probably didn't want to stray to far from that.

They both were real, natural, characters. It seemed that they could go for a week without talking to anyone other than what was necessary on their jobs.

Willie and Billy. They could have been called Dumb and Dumber. What one didn't think of to do that didn't make sense, the other one wouldn't disappoint you. One winter, they put antifreeze in their birdbath in the back yard "to keep the water open" for the birds. They killed a good share of visiting birds with that one.

The neighborhood kids always wanted to go over to their place to see what they were going to do next. No one wanted to ever poke fun at them, just watch for them to do something "different."

One winter, they were ice fishing on Green Bay out from the Menominee Lloyd Factory. There were a lot of other fishermen out there and most everyone tried different ways to fish. The fish seemed to be active in about 20-30 feet of water.

It was a long pull to get them up. If you could do it quickly, you had a chance of catching another perch or herring as they traveled in "schools" or groups down there. The fish holes were all hand-drilled through, normally, one to two and a half feet of ice.

One person out there, rigged up a bicycle wheel on a stand (without the tire). He wound one fish line to the right around it and one line to the left around it. When one line was down, the other was then wound up. When he'd get a fish on, he'd "spin the wheel" and the fish would come up quickly. The wet line would freeze from the cold air but it was easy to manage on the wheel.

The other line, wound in reverse, would automatically then, be lowered down the hole for catching a second fish as quick as possible. That was one of the slickest rigs that I ever saw on the Bay.

One big problem for everyone was that the cold temperatures would constantly cause the fishing holes to freeze. A coating of ice would form in no time. It had to constantly be removed with a strainer so the line didn't freeze into it. Most everyone tried something different to combat this. One fisherman poured alcohol into his fish hole to keep it open. Most of the guys that I saw out there, drank any alcohol they had and it was considered a true waste to put any into the hole.

Willie and Billy fished there regularly. They had the same line problem as everyone else. One day, they brought some car drain-oil out there with them. They poured that into their hole to prevent it from freezing over. That part WORKED except ……… whenever they pulled their line up through that drain oil, it became coated with heavy, black, oil AS DID THEIR FISH!

The other fishermen, naturally, crowded over to watch this. I could hear, "Hey, guys, you've got to see this….." Everyone was careful not to noticeably poke fun at them, though. They were both about 250 pounds of solid muscle. Short of some things, but not on solid muscle. No one wanted to get them mad. This was a long way from the shore and no place to hide.

Some of the other fishermen were sitting on their pails, watching them out of the corner of their eyes. You could see their shoulders jumping up and down as they were laughing, inwardly.

One local tavern used to pour the "returned, half-empty, beer mugs into what looked like a plastic, five-quart ice cream bucket. He'd refrigerate it and keep filling it until one or both of the boys came in. He'd then give it to them, free. They'd drink it down. Normally, they did this all in one lift of the bucket. The local guys would wait to watch that, too. The Wild West had nothing over some of the things that went on in Menominee.

Another time, a two-year-old neighbor boy was visiting at their house with his mother. The little guy was eating dry Frosted Flakes (cereal) in a small dish. He held one out for the cat to eat. The cat was sitting on the floor, smelled the Frosted Flakes but made no effort to open its mouth to eat it. The little guy was starting to cry and getting frustrated as the cat wouldn't open its mouth and eat the cereal.

Willie saw this. He said, "Let me help you." He slowly walked over and stepped on the cat's tail…..hard! That cat opened its mouth big enough to reach in and set a Frosted Flake onto its tonsil! It let out a "Yah-Hoooooo!" loud enough to be heard a block away. Willie smiled and sat back down. He felt that he had done a good thing.

Another time, some desperate prisoners escaped from the Marquette State Prison. The state police set up roadblocks on the three bridges connecting Marinette and Menominee. The Menominee River is wide and has a natural border.

That evening, after dark, for some reason, Willie and Billy started to walk across the middle bridge along its sidewalk. A few of us kids, were down there watching the excitement, hoping the prisoners would come so we'd see some real action!

Then, we notice Willie and Billy. We told the state trooper to check these guys out. They were walking through the roadblock. The trooper raised his shotgun and told them to "Halt!" The boys both looked at that shotgun and walked a little faster. As they walked, they said, "We didn't do nothing, so we're not stopping" and they kept right on walking across the bridge.

Now, that state trooper was something kind of special in Menominee during these times. No one in Menominee saw them very often. Their impressive uniform, special squad car, and special authority. Someone greater than the local police.

The trooper was losing ground with these guys. His authority was being challenged and he wanted to regain it. He worked the shotgun's slide-pump for effect and told them to "Stop or suffer the consequences!"

Willie and Billy were not impressed. I think it was Willie that said, "We didn't do nothing and you better not give us any trouble!" The trooper looked like he was quickly sizing up his options. He'd literally have to wrestle these guys or shoot them to get them to stop. He probably thought that even if he shot them, they looked like they'd still choke him before they died. He lowered his shotgun and said to us, "You kids, get out of here. This is a dangerous place."

We figured, it sure is. If he had pushed Willie and Billy a little more, they probably would have tipped over his car.

As kids, we'd go over to their house, see them in the yard or garage and ask, "What are you going to do today, Willie and Billy?" They'd slowly look at you, sometimes narrow their eyes, and if they didn't give you an answer by then, you knew not to ask again. They were always happy and "Doing their own thing." An example, if possibly a new stop sign was put up on some corner, most drivers would stop for it, some may slowly coast through it, Willie and Billy might just bring that stop sign home.

They seemed to outsmart the local game warden whenever they'd go hunting. Or, maybe that game warden was smarter than we thought and didn't want to confront them. Anyone who did would have been considered that they like to "Live on the edge."

They always brought home some type of game to eat. Once, it looked like they shot 3-4 chickens. They had these dead chickens in the back seat of their car. They carried them into the house by the legs like one would carry a limit of partridge.

Strangers never heard of guys like this when they would come to a city. The Chamber of Commerce never talked about them like they would about some other citizens. Although, every community seems to have one special character where you grew up, we were lucky. We had Willie and Billy.

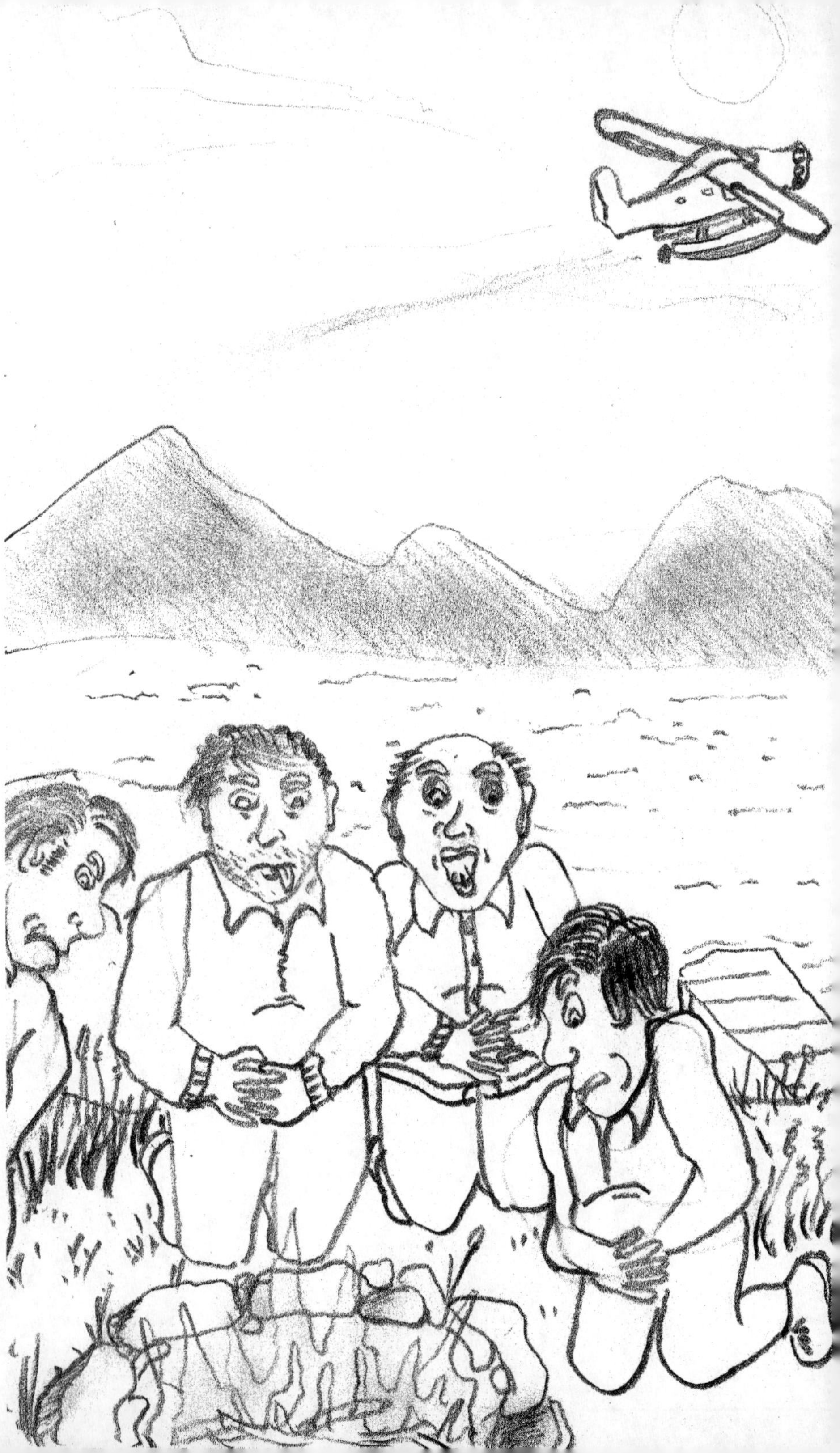

CHAPTER 10

WE ALMOST DIED!!
A NEAR DISASTER FISHING EXPERIENCE

This is a true story about one of my good friends, Romy. He and his fishing crew of three others came close to seeing the Pearly Gates on this trip.

They drove up to Wawa, Ontario this particular June to be flown into a remote trout lake for four days. They arrived on time, as this was an annual routine trip for them (same place that we go a week later).

Romy owns one of the nicest supper clubs on Kelly Lake in Oconto County, Wisconsin. It's not the nicest because it's expensive, elegant, or high class. It's the nicest because of Romy's personality to everyone and the friendly crowd that he attracts (he'd make a good Yooper).

You can imagine a lot of hunters and fishermen there, but also people like my wife (bless her), like to go there and she doesn't hunt or fish. He says that it's a tense job to satisfy everyone (weddings, Duck's Unlimited, all other parties) but to me, he seems to thrive on it. He told me that he really looks forward to "relaxing in Canada" on these fishing trips.

This one started off normal enough. There is no regular drinking water near this remote cabin. You can boil the lake water for coffee but otherwise, the fishermen bring in beer and pop to substitute for the drinking water.

I might tell you that Romy's crew appreciates their beer. Especially that Canadian beer. The pilot told me that when he flies them in, he thinks the plane's tail goes under the water for a while when the pontoons touch the lake surface on the landing because of the extra beer that these guys take along.

They were fishing brook trout on this trip. The small lake that they land on has nothing but brook trout in it. When you get a bite, it's always a trout.

There is only one old cabin on the whole lake. The Outfitter has some type of contract with the Province that he leases it for so many years and in turn can put up one cabin and no one else has cabin or fly-in rights to the lake.

You should know that the cabin is very old and many mice took up residence there. One guy with Romy cringed and said, "I hate mice!" Romy told him, happily, "Better the mice than a snake. If you see mice, we know there's no snakes here. They would have eaten the mice." With that happy thought, they settled in their sleeping bags on the bunks, groceries on the shelf, and set out some De-Con that they brought with.

I asked him if he had a good crew on this trip. He said, "Yeah. This one guy is "starting to hide his own Easter Eggs, but otherwise is pretty normal." The trip was four days of fishing before the plane would return and take them back out.

It was a warm, June week. Fishing was good the first three days and everything was going well. Loons were landing in close to the cabin in the evening. Their sounds, the warm nights, the stars sprinkled all over the sky, fish jumping on the lake surface after evening bugs, a cool beer, all made perfect evenings to sit on the porch and just say, "It doesn't get any better than this."

The fourth day was something else!! Everyone was sick! Not little sick but BIG TIME sick! He said, "We were dizzy, off-balance, were up-chucking, couldn't control ourselves and were to weak to get out of our sleeping bags. Our systems were out of control. I had a brand-new sleeping bag and had the diarrhea bad. That bag was full of it. We weren't sure what happened to us."

We should have suspected something with the cooking when we saw a mouse go near the frying pan on the stove, walk away wobbly and die. "That frying pan was killing them as good as the De-Con."

We were supposed to fly out at noon that day and there wasn't one of us strong enough to stand up. At noon, he crawled out in the front clearing to the plane dock. The other guys also were starting to crawl around. At this point, we felt like we were dying but didn't know from what. We were even having a hard time thinking and reasoning.

The plane could be heard coming closer and soon was skimming over the lake. He said, "I was crawling on my hands and knees and waved to the plane. The pilot flew by the dock, saw us crawling around, touched the water like a football drop kick, waved, and was airborne. He just flew away................."

Later, the pilot told them, he assumed that they were all "shinned up" from the beer and didn't want to be responsible to take them up and possibly have someone fall out of the plane. Can you imagine being that close to help and watch it leave you?

They crawled down into the lake and laid there with just their heads out for a couple of hours. It helped to get their body temperature down closer to normal. After a lot of suffering, cleaning up and rest, they were somewhat back to normal.

They reasoned that it was food poisoning. They had used the same fish grease in the pan for two days in the heat.

The next day, the plane returned and the pilot apologized many times over, never realizing that they were truly sick. Romy said, "We put a couple of extra bucks in the church collection the next Sunday. I'd never want to go through that experience again!"
Did they ever go back? Right away the next summer but he said everyone washed the dishes right after they ate.

GRUNT
SNORT
GRUNT

CHAPTER 11

"BEAR TRACKS!"

We were fishing, this summer, in the Huron Mountains near Lake Superior. Most people probably don't know that there are bonafide mountains in Michigan's U.P.

I'm sure, we came in the "back door" to get into this area. We went through the L'Anse Reservation, Skanee, and some near-impassable sand roads.

We were really "back there," Bill and I, my favorite fishing partner. A rugged and untamed as this country looked, the brook trout streams that we found also looked "untapped." There was no sign of other fishermen, campers, or loggers in the near, 10-mile area.

We figured that we'd set up camp by a nice looking trout stream. There was a large sand clearing, a beautiful looking trout stream with rapids, pools, rushing water, plenty of firewood, and "BEAR TRACKS!" Fresh bear tracks!

Bill said, "What do you think?" "If there's fresh bear tracks around, it must be good fishing," I said. He looked back at me squinting his eyes like he was acting as brave as I sounded. We rigged up our poles and started fishing on that stream or river. We weren't sure what it was. It was about 20-30 feet across, in spots, a lot of small rapids and those unmistakable bear tracks up and down the banks.

After fishing for a while, we checked the time. It was about 2:00 p.m. and the trout were biting quick and hard. It seemed that every pool below small rapids or around a corner of the stream where a huge rock blocked half of the stream had hungry trout.

In an hour, we had plenty to eat. Real native brookies. Deep red in color, they ran about 8 to 11 inches. Nice eating size.

Bill cleaned the fish while I fried up some potatoes and made coffee. He came up the 10-foot high bank and said, "I'll tell you, those bear tracks down there in the sand, look as fresh as ours do." We passed that off and ate a mouth-watering meal of fresh trout, fried potatoes, beans heated in their own can, and fresh coffee.

We cleaned up our dishes and went back to the car and slept. We were tired from driving many miles from Menominee to get to this area. The fresh air and that nice meal seemed to put us to sleep with a smile.

When we awoke, it was getting noticeably dark. We had a 7 x 7 wall tent for sleeping. The evening was so nice though, that we decided to just set up our army cots and sleep under the stars. A famous first for us. There were no mosquitoes as we were in a clearing with a breeze.

We DID have an automatic .22 rifle with us. I loaded it up and placed it within reach under my cot. We never thought that we'd need it, but, hey! It gave you a feeling of some security and we DID see a lot of those bear tracks.

Bill said, "You keep the gun. I'm not too concerned about the bear." I lay there on my cot, looking up at the stars and smiled. I remembered one happening last year. We were driving home after dark from hunting partridge by Shakey Lakes (Lake Township). I was driving and Bill was on the passenger's side. I turned a corner on country highway 577 and there was a big, black bear sitting in the road. His eyes were shinning bright red in the headlights. It then walked into the dark woods off of the road. Bill quickly said, "Let me out and you shine the headlights into the woods where it went. I'd like to see it again. I'm not afraid of a bear."

I did just that, for a few minutes……. Then, I figured, let's see how brave he really is. I slipped the car into gear and started down the road. I looked to the right and in the headlights, I swear that he was outrunning the car. So much for being brave.

The night was peaceful. No mosquitoes, the stars were out, the fire was burning its last glow of light, and it was getting plenty dark. You could barely make out the shape of the car that was parked not too far away.

Contrary to what one reads in those national outdoor sports magazines, one does not fall asleep quickly from this, quiet, secluded, peaceful, and natural setting. NOOOOOOOOO! Your ears hear every snapping of a tree limb, wings of the night birds, and your always listening for any strange sounds. You have to exhaust yourself like this before you drop off to sleep.

The fire was flickering its last gasp of light, bright then dim, a little glow, then dimmer. My eyes were getting relaxed and I was just ready to sleep. THEN IT HAPPENED! Twigs started to snap outside of our campsite. We could hear a grunting sound coming from the brush-snapping noise. Then, everything was quiet, again.

I whispered to Bill, "Did you hear that?" He said, "Yeeeyah!" He had the only flashlight. In seconds, he was shinning it all around the woods where we heard the sounds. Being that HE had the flashlight, I quickly thought, he might make a dash for the car and even lock the door (remembering the treatment that I gave him last year on highway 577 in Lake Township).

After a while, he said, "I think it was a deer. Let's go to sleep." He shut off the light and everything was quiet. Then, things happened fast! The grunting started again. It kept coming closer and closer! The brush was cracking louder. There was no time to even get out of your blankets.

It was now right inside our campsite circle of the car, two cots, and the burned-out fire. "Ooofff"! "Ooofff," "Ooofff," "Ooofff," and LOUD! I started to slowly, slowly (it seemed like slow motion when your ready for something to pounce on you) reach for the .22.

The "Oooofff," "Oooofff," was now right alongside of me. In the near dark, I could see something moving by the side of my cot where I was reaching. I told Bill to shine the light by my cot, QUICK! I also started wondering why he didn't have the light on sooner or, how far down into his blankets did he go?

He shinned the light by my cot and THANK GOD, I didn't reach down any further. There was a huge porcupine grunting and waddling around under my cot! We scared it away, took a deep breath and quickly set up the tent to finish our nights sleep. We could hear the porky come back later, grunting and brushing against the outside of the tent, looking for something to eat.

In the morning, we were fixing breakfast and getting ready to go fishing again. We couldn't believe what we saw! A cloud of road dust and a station wagon full of kids and their parents came bouncing down the road.

The father rolled down his window (a real tourist-looking type, with city clothes) and asked if this was the highest point in Michigan? Bill said, "Oh, no. See that highest hill over there? That's it. That's the spot." The father smiled, put away his road map, and said, "Everyone out." He had some deep obsession to climb to the highest point in Michigan.

Bill knew that there was no way in God's green earth that HE would climb that densely timbered, tangle-foot of a high hill. There was not even an animal trail up there. He was fascinated to see how this guy planned on doing it, especially, with his family.

First, they had to cross that stream. It was about two feet deep there. There were rocks sticking out that one could jump from one to the other, but…….. you realize, ……. Every rock isn't evenly spaced an equal distance apart.

His wife and older kids crossed with no trouble. His one younger daughter had one foot on one rock and one foot on another. These were too far apart for her. She looked like she was doing the "split." He thought for a second, then wadded out into knee deep water and took her to the far shore. Now, his shoe and socks were squishy wet as were his pants. They all then, disappeared into the woods in the direction of that high, well-bushed, ridge of probably, mosquitoes and tangle-foot.

Bill said, "We better wait here until they come back. I feel a little guilty with that bunch free in the woods." After about two hours, they came back. Most of them had torn clothes, were scratching mosquito bites like crazy and talking to themselves. The guy said to Bill, "How come there's no sign of other tourists up there if that's the highest point in Michigan?"

Bill said, "That's the highest point around here, but there is another one. They call it Brockway Mountain Drive. You can drive on it with your car. You should be able to find it on that map you have there."

The father started shouting something at his wife then. She said, "Just get in the car and get us out of here before these mosquitoes eat us up." They then turned the car around and bounced out of there. "Some people do the oddest things on their vacations," Bill said, shaking his head. We never did see any bear on that trip......

CHAPTER 12

EARLY RAINBOW RUN
ON THE BIG HURON RIVER

The locals called them "Steelheads" and some just called them big rainbow. These are trout that come up the Big Huron River from Lake Superior, in the spring of the year.

This is located in the U.P. near L'Anse and Skanee. I was lucky enough to get in on a weeklong trip with nine other guys from Menominee. They needed one more person to hold the front end of a boat down in the water. They had made this trip before so they were all set up for it.

We drove up to the mouth of the Huron River in a caravan of five cars towing five 14-foot boats. I can't remember how long it took us to get there but I do remember that we were all really tired when we got there.

Most of the last roads were gravel, then down to sand, then to a one-lane grass and sand road. It was getting dark when we finally got there. Without the experience that the other guys had from being there last year, one wouldn't have known where THERE was.

They set up a tent just big enough for all of us to sleep in shoulder to shoulder. Then two bales of loose straw were thrown around on the floor with a canvas tarp spread over it. You placed your sleeping bag over that, and you were on your own.

There were fresh bear tracks in the sand on the campsite when we arrived. Everyone seemed to be understandably looking over his shoulder as we put up that tent. We were the only sign of human activity in the last 40 miles.

That night, we were all lying shoulder to shoulder in the tent. Most fell asleep quickly. Most SNORED loudly. In fact, it seemed to me, that the tent walls were being "sucked in," then, "bellied out," as they inhaled and exhaled.

After about two hours of no sleep, I raised the side of the tent, dragged my sleeping bag about 30 feet from the tent, put on my cap with the ear flaps down, and fell asleep. The cold air was welcomed compared to the snoring. Sometime in the middle of the night, there was shouting in the tent and flashlights flashing around into the woods.

Someone saw that my sleeping bag was gone and the side of the tent was loose. They thought that a bear probably dragged it out of the tent. I couldn't help but notice that they showed a little more respect toward me, the youngest fisherman, after sleeping outside while they were huddled together in the tent.

Lake Superior was on one side of our campsite by about a 100 yards and the Big Huron River was about 30 yards on the other. We tied the boats along the riverbank. The main plan was to motor into Lake Superior and troll-fish about 75 yards parallel to the shore. We trolled back and forth across the river's mouth.

An orange flatfish with black dots was the best bait. The first morning out, each boat seemed to average 2-4 fish. That probably doesn't sound like many, but they were huge. The size was running from 14 to 28 inches. That's a nice trout to catch on lighter line with a spinning reel.

The Huron was at near flood-stage. It is a very winding river with many turns, deep holes, undercut banks from the fast spring current, sandbars, and in places, a lot of fast, white water. There was a sandbar extending out into the river at about every third bend. Most of them had fresh bear tracks on them.

The other guys knew about two 14-foot diameter, "logging wheels" upstream in the center of the river. They wanted to check and see if they were still there. The water, in that area, was crystal clear. You could see every detail of those wheels perfectly. They were down in about 10 feet of water. They were left over from the early historic logging days. Horses would pull logs out of difficult swamps using these high wheels. One could only guess, how many years they were preserved on that river bottom.

We traveled up the river about a mile and met a REAL native. This guy looked like he slept in the woods. When he stood still, he blended right in with all of his faded clothes.

He had dragged an old, wooden, homemade (from one-inch lumber), boat out of the grass and had it on a sandbar by the river. We stopped and watched him caulk it with old rags and a knife. After a couple of hours, he attached an old motor that he had hiding in the woods.

The motor had no handle on it. Nothing to steer it with. He started it up, put his arm around it to steer it, and headed downstream to go into Lake Superior. He was bailing water out steady, as he was going.

We couldn't believe that anyone would take that boat into Lake Superior, so we followed and watched him. It was unbelievable! He entered Lake Superior and steered straight out like he was going to Canada. We thought that the guy was a little crazy or one, real, Yooper! One or two good "thuds" of the waves on the bottom of that boat could have knocked the caulking out. We watched him until he went out of sight.

The next day, we were going to take the cars upstream about 10 miles to a road that the guys found years before. The DNR had a lamprey weir across the river there, so the lamprey couldn't go upstream.

The trout also wanted to go upstream and they were also held back by the electric currents from that weir. We fished for them with barbless hooks (we cut the barb off) so they weren't injured when we threw them back. They bite like crazy. We kept enough for a meal and released the rest. They were mostly in the 10-13 inch size. Nice eating.

By the third day, everyone was tired of eating fish. We caught many more in Lake Superior by just trolling offshore from the river's mouth. We got up for a later-than-usual breakfast. Wes looked into the big coffeepot to check how hot it was. He shouted, "Someone sh—in the coffeepot!" The cook laughed until he had tears in his eyes. He had broken two eggs in with the coffee. That is supposed to collect any floating grounds, etc., and leave clear coffee.

It DID look like something unusual floating in there. It didn't hold anyone back from drinking the coffee, though.

The next year, I was recalled into the army, so I never did get in on that trip again. That early spring fishing probably petered out just like our smelt fishing seems to have, over the years.

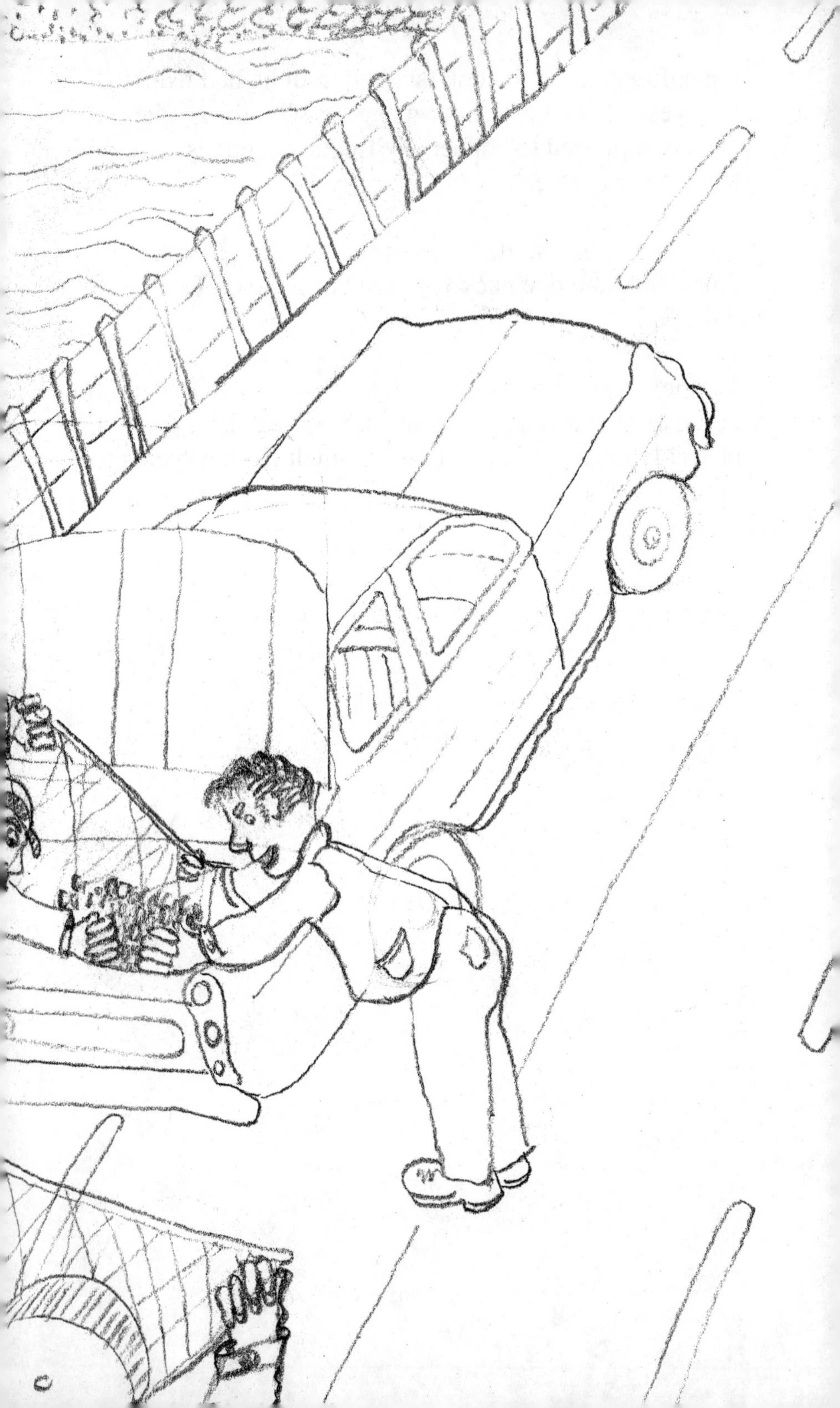

CHAPTER 13

SMELT FISHING ... WHERE HAVE ALL THE SMELT GONE?

Growing up in Menominee, one of the spring rituals was always smelt fishing. As soon as the ice went off of the Menominee River and most of Green Bay, the suckers have their yearly spawning "run" upstream.

There is no limit on the amount one can keep. A spring caught sucker properly smoked, taste as good as the best of any smoked chubs.

Then one to two weeks after the "Sucker Run," the "Smelt Run" would always start upstream into the rivers and streams, ditches, emptying into Green Bay, Lake Michigan, and Lake Superior.

As teenagers, and later as young adults, my brother and I would go down to the Hattie Street Bridge between Marinette and Menominee to anxiously watch for signs of the Smelt Run to begin. At the first sign of "Smelt action," we'd make the necessary repairs to our long-handled dip net (the netting always need annual repairs), take a few pails with us, and walk the four blocks from our house to "get in on the action."

Smelt season was always an exciting time. Years ago, in Menominee, they would elect a Smelt Queen with the normal festivities. There was live wrestling, where the wrestlers would wrestle in 6 inches to one foot of smelt (similar to Jello wrestling, now).

There are three main bridges and one train bridge between Marinette and Menominee. As smelt normally "run" the best after dark, all those bridges would be lit up by Coleman lanterns from many, many fishermen either with drop nets from the bridges or scoop nets under the bridges. All along the shores there would be bright fires made from wood scraps and old tires for light and heat, in case someone fell in.

As teenagers, this was the place to be, if you were from Marinette or Menominee. The teenage boys would all be fishing and teenage girls would naturally, follow at a safe distance. When the "run" was on, all of the boys would be really busy. They would tell the girls, if you want to stay with the boys, they had to bite the head off of a live smelt. SOME WOULD ACTUALLY DO IT!

Our favorite spot to "dip net" was always under the Hattie Street bridge. There was a natural channel there, close to the shore. One year, the fishermen were spaced about five feet apart all across the bridge with "drop nets" from the bridge above. A "drop net" is a square net about four feet square made out of a one inch pipe frame with a regular mesh net attached to the frame. The weight of the pipe will drop it to the river bottom. It has a strong rope attached (each corner to a center rope) to pull the net up and to drop it back down.

Our set-up was always a pair of hip boots to "go out farther," dip net and a pail to put the smelt in. On a good night, one scoop with that long handled net would bring in a half pail of smelt. To get down under that bridge used to be a challenge in itself. There was no walkway or city planning done that fishermen should go there.

There was a strong, cyclone fence that ran downhill to the river's edge allowing about four feet wide of space between the bridge and the fence to walk down to the water. This "walkway" was a mixture of huge slabs of cement dumped in there for fill, to prevent erosion. They were all irregular sizes. One step would be about a foot drop and the next probably about a three-foot drop before the next step, etc. You had to hang on to that cyclone fence, your equipment, and feel with your foot for the next foothold in the dark.

We'd fill the pails quickly and sometime, take them upon the bridge to sell to the stranger driving through. Any strangers driving through whom saw this action for the first time, really were excited. Of course, most of them had to buy some smelt to take home. They sold for 25¢ a pail full during the "peak of the run" as they were so plentiful.

We were about ready to go back home one night, when four guys stopped with a brand new Buick Roadmaster. It was so new that you could smell the "newness" inside. They were from Illinois and had never seen anything like a Smelt Run before. They were also "feeling no pain" from a night of sharing "good spirits" somewhere, together.

They insisted that we catch them 8 to 10 pails of smelt. They were going to take them all home and share them with friends. A couple of bucks was big money to us, then. We dipped our pails full for them and asked where their containers were to put them in.

They had this new car and that was it …. One of them opened the car's trunk. There was only a new spare tire and the trunk liner that was immaculately clean. He said, "Pour them in there. We'll take them out when we get home." We smiled and poured 10 pails of smelt into that new car's trunk. The fish were sliding down into the spare wheel well, down the sides of the trunk and a huge mound filling the center of the trunk (until you can imagine, when they put on the breaks on their way home.)

They were all so happy that they got such a "cheap deal" that they thanked us and drove away. We wondered if they remembered that those fish were even in their trunk the next day. What a way to "break in" a new car.

Another time, we were dipping in that same spot when six big guys came down there and literally pushed us out of that good spot with their waders and moved right in front of us. It was useless to stay as that was the one and only good fishing spot down there. They had no regard for us except to move us out.

It was nearly 11:00 p.m. and plenty dark down there. You couldn't see the irregular walkway anymore because of the dark without a flashlight. If you had a flashlight, you wouldn't have wanted to see where you had to go. We knew our way around from past experience, so we began the task of hanging onto that fence, pulling ourselves uphill on that irregular pile of cement slabs that we used for steps.

When we got to the top, my brother said, "There has to be some way that we can return the favor to those guys that pushed us out of our fishing hole." He smiled, "Let's pour these smelt onto those steps down below." We poured about 10 gallons of slippery smelt onto that already near-impossible path of concrete that we called "steps".

When you looked down the irregular concrete, below was just white with those slippery, slimy, smelt. I can't imagine how they carried any amount of fish up that trail. We walked home, smiling, feeling that justice was served.

Now, this year, as I'm writing this, there is not even any talk about a Smelt Run. They seem to have disappeared or are being eaten up by larger fish. There were so many, many thousands of them during a normal Smelt run that it seemed impossible for these spring runs to ever end.

Ruleau's (commercial fishermen in Menominee) is running a trawler out of Two Rivers, Wisconsin for smelt. They are doing reasonable well and supplying the local market. It's easier to buy them at the store and they taste the same, however, the adventure is not there compared to being by that rushing. Spring water, the bonfires, and Coleman lanterns for light blazing up and down the river. Or feeling the "ping, ping, ping" of many smelt literally hitting against your hip boots as they were swimming upstream in the dark river, or the excitement of the crowd in the air. Smelt Runs were always exciting times.

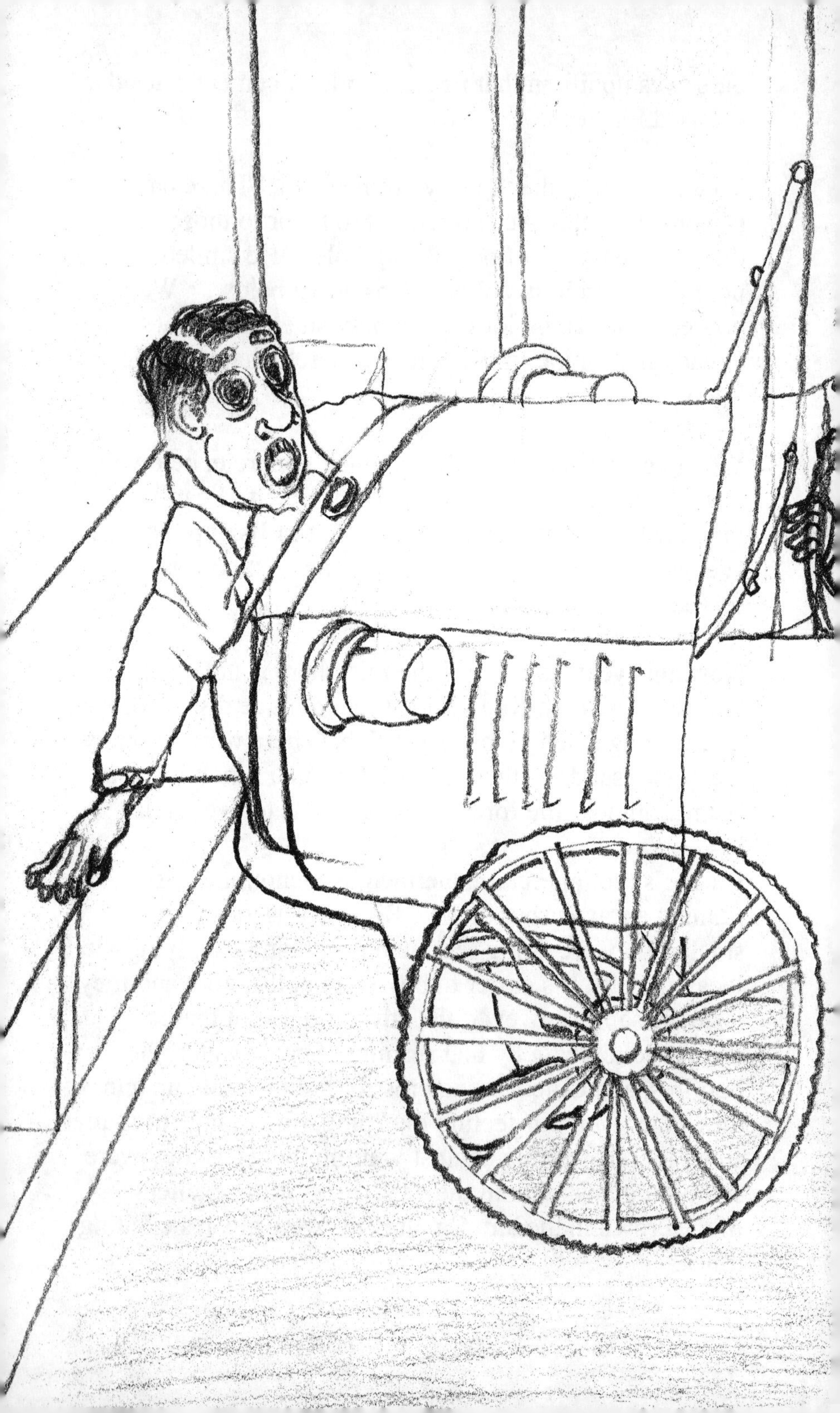

CHAPTER 14

AN UNFORGETTABLE CHARACTER JOE ST. JOHN

Joe was a neighbor of ours in Menominee where I grew up. He lived about three empty lots away. Most people, by nature, stayed away from Joe. He never walked a straight line. Whatever he did, he was always looking over his shoulder first.

The neighbors said that Joe loved three things in life; his wife, drinking, and his pigs, but they weren't sure in what order.

He was a hard worker in a local factory during the week but on weekends, as other people went to church religiously, Joe drank religiously. He would drink with a buddy who'd give him a ride "almost" home on Friday night. Joe still had to walk a full two blocks to his house down a gravel road from where he was "let off." I think Joe's buddy was as scared of Joe's wife as he was.

There were no houses on that road so Joe would stop ½ to rest. There was a huge, sloped, stone up against a telephone pole about ½ way so Joe would stop there and sit on that sloped stone to rest before he'd continue on home. He'd look a little odd sitting with one leg extended up in the air and the other hanging down as he would lean against the telephone pole. That was also the natural slope of how that stone was set.

One day, he told the neighborhood kids that he swore he saw a real, live, fairy sitting on that stone. Thereafter, everyone called it, Joe's Fairy Stone.

He always wore a pair of bib-overalls and a blue work shirt. He was a skinny guy so the sides of the overalls (where they had a single button on each side) kind of flopped back and forth as he walked. If he went to a party and needed to dress up, he'd wear a new pair of overalls and a new blue shirt. He must have had one set that he saved for special occasions.

Joe had a small, modest house. It had a back screen door with no screen in the bottom half. He usually had a piece of plywood fitted there over all the years. Sometimes, for whatever reason, there was nothing there. I never was inside of his house. Joe would always "come outside" to talk whenever anyone would come over.

His garage was big enough for a workbench in front and the car almost tight to the workbench and to the garage door.

Joe was a welder by trade so his workbench was made out of heavy angle iron all welded together. One weekend, Joe decided that he wanted to put his car, a Model A Ford, into the garage but didn't trust himself to drive it in (he had already done his "religious thing" for the weekend). He told his son, Terry, to get behind the wheel and he'd guide him in. Joe said, "You can do it, boy. Just watch my directions."

Terry was beside himself. He actually had "permission" to fool with the car. He was too young to know how to drive but Joe felt he couldn't do any harm if he watched Joe's directions. With a Model A, if you stepped on the starter and had it in gear, it would lurch ahead about 2-3 feet. Then step on the starter again and it would keep repeating the cycle.

Joe showed him the basics and was all set to go. He got in front of the car and motioned it in with both hands. Terry had a smile from ear to ear and his eyes were opened wider than normal as he gripped the wheel.

Joe looked as confident as a General giving orders to the troops. "Easy, easy, over to the right, easy, easy." Finally, Terry got the car in by stepping on the starter and letting it lurch ahead. Joe forgot about the workbench in front of the car and behind him. Suddenly, Terry had him pinned against that angle iron bench and the car radiator. Joe's eyes were bulging and his head was resting on top of the radiator looking at Terry, like a hood ornament. He was caught tight against the bench.

Through crunched teeth and a near whisper, Joe said, "Easy, easy, back it up, easy, easy." Poor Terry only knew how to step on the starter. The bumper would flex and the workbench would push back a few inches each time the car jumped ahead.

Joe's wife finally saw the action and came out, shut the car off and left Joe to push his own way out. He didn't talk to anyone after that. He just went over and sat by his pig yard. His wife had a habit of locking him out when he did odd things like that.

Joe loved his pigs and like any other animal, he had his favorite pig. One Friday night, he came home singing loud enough so that the whole neighborhood knew Joe was "coming home." His wife saw him coming, weaving back and forth, so she promptly locked him out.

He then walked out to the pigpen and got out his favorite pig. Joe sat down against a fence post, one hand around the pig's neck and the other held his bottle. Soon, it was one for Joe and one for the pig.

The neighbors never knew what Joe was going to do next. One summer day, there was a huge cloud of dust coming down the gravel road. Here came Joe driving he Model A. He had a telephone pole attached by one end to a long, logging chain and to his back bumper. It would swing from one side of the road to the other raising more dust that 10 cars could have. He said that he found it and brought it home for firewood. It looked brand new. He must have spotted it on his way home from work.

One summer, Joe passed himself and a friend off as first class carpenters. They got a job finishing off the inside of a new house for a fellow moving north from Chicago. The guy showed up one hot summer day and was really impressed with their work. Joe didn't tell him that the original carpenter did the work, he was so impressed with.

In fact, the guy was so pleased that he bought a small barrel of beer and a tap. He told Joe that they could enjoy it after their workday and then he left. Joe couldn't believe it!! He looked across the room at that keg, shocked, like he was looking at the Second Coming of

Christ. He couldn't believe anyone would give him a keg of beer and say, "Go to it, Joe."

His partner caught up with his work, said, "What do we nail next, Joe?" Joe said, with a smile, "We're going to nail that keg." And so they did. Joe slept on that house floor all night.

Joe always moved slowly when he walked. He always said that life was too short to hurry through it. Another time, Joe came home singing and feeling no pain. His wife, again, promptly locked the front screen door. We watched to see what he'd do next.

Joe kind of cocked his head to one side sizing up the door. He then backed up about 40 feet and put his head down and dove through the glass storm door. His wife seemed so surprised and probably figured that if he loved her that much to come in that she let him stay inside.

He always told us how lucky he was. If his wife were mad at him, the pigs would always be happy to see him. I always thought that when he went to their pen and they were jumping against the fence, it was because they were hungry. Joe sometimes forgot to feed them. He would say, "What a life, boys ……….. The pigs, my wife, and a little beer …… who would want more?"

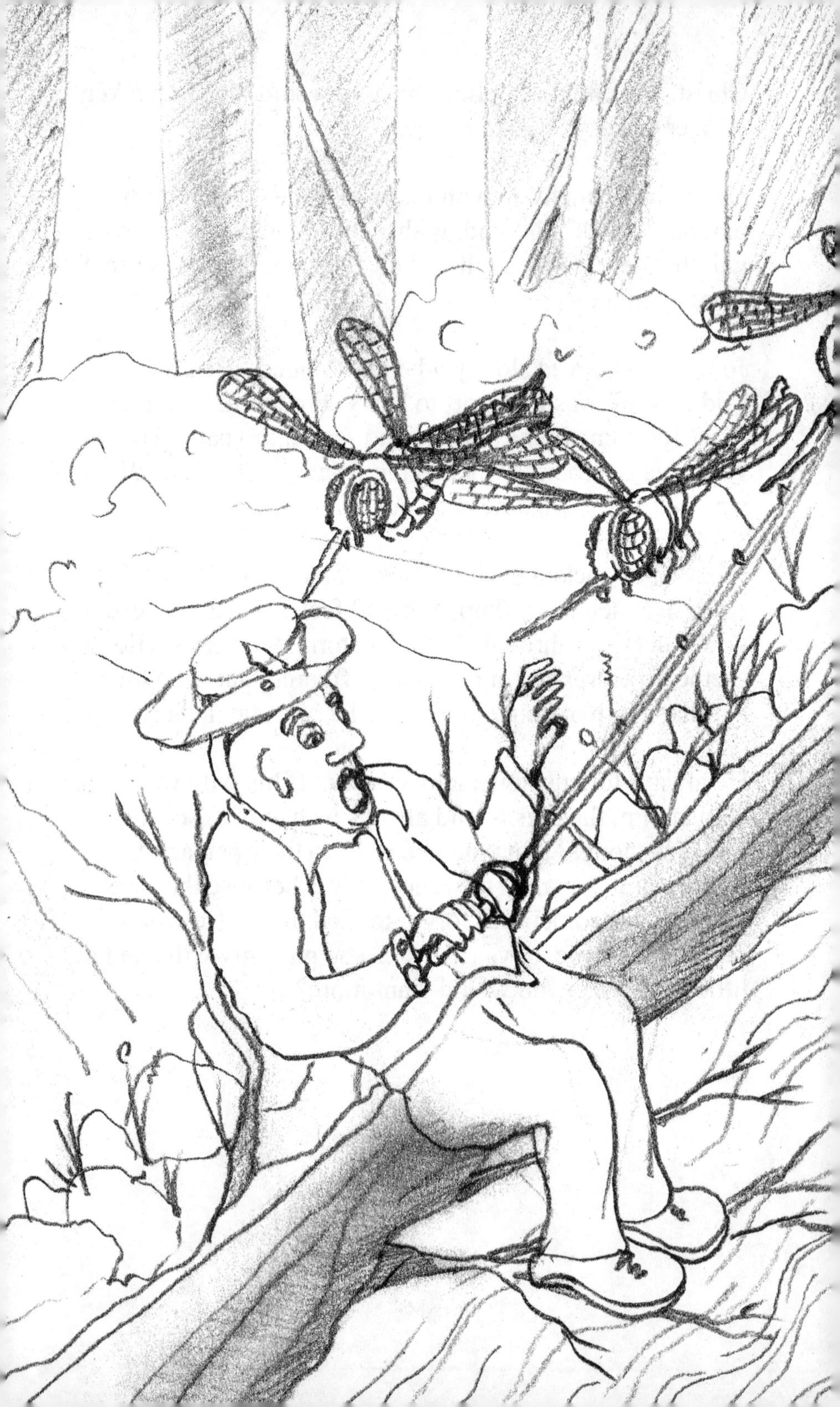

CHAPTER 15

MOSQUITOES AS BIG AS HUMMING BIRDS

I saw a bumper sticker this month that said, "The U.P. has two seasons, shoveling and swatting." Most of us, up here, take it so much for granted that we do these things without a second thought. I was stream fishing for brook trout with my friends, Bill and Ben last month. We drove up to fish a stretch of the Ford River near Ralph.

With all of the every other day rain we were getting, the back roads weren't in too good of shape. We stopped in the general area where we normally fished in the past, I waited for Ben who usually jumped out of the car first to check the river conditions for fishing. He was pulling on the door handle but not opening the door. I said, "What's up?" Ben said, "Holy Wah! The mosquitoes are so thick that I can't get the door open."

There were clouds of them and they were friends of no one. Some that I saw looked like they had hair on their chest. When you rolled down the window, they were buzzing so loud that they sounded like bees. We had the good sense to "dope up" with mosquito spray before we got out of the car. They were really thick! Ben said that

they were so thick that he could lean on them while he put on his hip boots so he didn't get off-balance.
Our plan was to fish upstream to a spring hole we knew about and set a six-pack of beer in there to cool. We'd meet there on our way out and have a few cool ones together. Other than the constant buzzing, the mosquitoes getting behind your glasses, picking off wood ticks as we moved through the brush, we did start to catch a few fish.

I never saw anything like it! Back at our fishing camp, those mosquitoes were hanging onto the porch screen by the 100's. Going to the outhouse was a big decision to make and then, and ordeal. They were so numerous that when you came back running from your "duty," you looked like you had a fur coat on. The constant rains had made perfect breeding conditions for this bumper crop. They weren't biting through our spray and lotion but they were getting on our nerves by their huge swarm hovering and buzzing around us.

Ben said that he'd fish the spring hole and we could each fish a different side of the river upstream. Bill and I were moving upstream picking up a few trout as we went. Then, I heard Bill taking to himself? I shouted to him to see if there was a problem. He said, "These damn mosquitoes! I kill one and 100 more come to his funeral." I encouraged him to keep it up. Maybe more would migrate that way.

We met about 500 yards farther upstream. Bill said, "What did we get into? I'm scratching like crazy, the spray wore off and they're coming through. I can't ever remember being this full of wood ticks. I keep picking them off and they keep climbing on." I asked how that new lotion he bought was working? "That Skin-So-Soft? I think they like it. Some of the bigger ones just flew off with the bottle." I hoped he was exaggerating.

We figured that we were fishing for about two hours and with the conditions mentioned, the fishing didn't seem all that important. We decided to go back to the spring hole, have a few cool ones, and head back to the place that advertised the "All-you-can-eat" chicken.

As we got closer to the spring hole, we could hear Ben talking. We noticed that he was sitting alone on the riverbank swatting mosquitoes with both hands and saying, "Mosquitoes as big as humming birds, they're as big as humming birds!"

He didn't look quite normal sitting there swatting and talking to himself. Bill was the first to notice all of the empty beer cans around him. He looked and said, "He didn't even save us ONE! We must have scared him with the look we both gave him because he said, "Don't look at me that way fellas. I did you a favor. You don't have to sit with these blasted mosquitoes and ticks like I did to drink that stuff."

He said, "I swear that I saw some mosquitoes as big as humming birds trying to get me. They had stingers two inches long! We noticed a humming bird nest near him and two humming birds but we didn't tell him. We figured part of his punishment for drinking our share could be worrying about those jumbo mosquitoes.

We got Ben back to the car and were all hot and hungry. Bill said, "We had better comb the wood ticks out of our hair and go for that 'All-you-can-eat' chicken." We told Ben that if he wanted to come in and eat, he had to stop talking about the "mosquitoes as big as humming birds!" because the poor guy was saying it like he really believed it.

We all ordered the "All-you-can-eat" chicken, as we hadn't eaten since breakfast. It now was 2:00 p.m. We had a few candy bars, of course, and Ben had our beer. We ate as hard as we fished. This was one job where we all knew what to do and there were no slackers.

After a while, we were all leaning back on our chairs content and satisfied. No pesky bugs bothering us. Ben said that he had to go to the restroom so we sat and waited for him. We could hear him explaining to some other customers in a booth about the mosquitoes, "as big as humming birds," that had stingers two inches long and they were after him. He looked so serious that as a stranger, you'd think that he was crazy or could have even seen the Second Coming of Christ. Being that the first was easier to believe, we nudged him out to the car and drove back home.

We laughed and figured that there was no one like his wife to straighten him out. She listened to very little to what he had to say and would tell him instantly what to do. I asked Bill when I let him off at his house, "What advice would you give any tourists that wanted to fish trout like we did today?" He thought for awhile and then said, "I'd tell them, stay on the main highway and buy their fish fry."

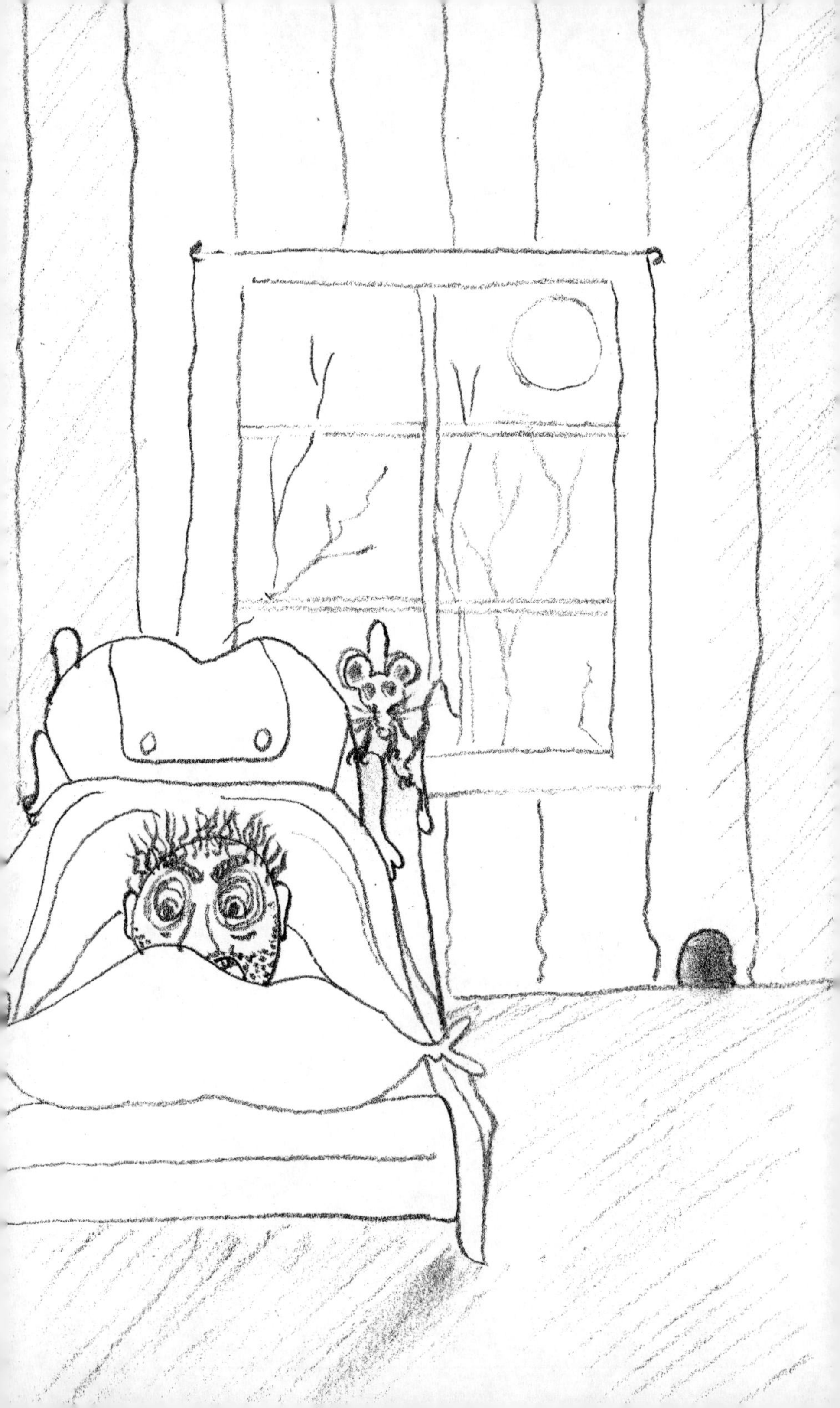

CHAPTER 16

THE TROUT CAMP

That's right, trout camp. The only excuse for this camp being, was to shelter trout fishermen. They say, if something is different from the normal, its got "character." If that's true, this camp had a lot of character.

It was a framed, well-faded, plywood camp that blended in well with the natural woods setting. It had holes in the high gable ends, about six inches round. A chipmunk would come in there, jump onto the rafters and chatter at us for a while and then leave.

We were a party of four fishermen using this remote cabin for a week's fishing on this trout lake in Canada. It was a fly-in trip so we were all alone for a week as it was the only cabin. The mice were the only permanent residents there. Bill said, "That's good. If we see a lot of mice, at least we know there are no snakes in here."

That was one comforting thought. I saw one, big, mouse staring me in the eye when I was stretched out to sleep. The mice were really plentiful. After we turned our Coleman lantern out the first night, the place seemed to be alive with them. You could hear them running on the rafters, the floor, and it sounded like they were trying to run up the walls.

Bill's mattress had a huge mouse hole in the side of it. He told us that he could feel mice running around in it. Everyone laughed at that, figuring that he was imagining things. Then he said, "Wah! That's not so bad. Now, I feel them bumping against my back. It feels like the 'magic fingers' on a vibrating bed in a Holiday Inn." He said that it relaxed him and he fell asleep better.

We thought, well, at least he's happy. The cabin had three wooden steps leading up to the front door. Dan was carrying an armful of wood up them on the second day and they collapsed. They broke into many pieces. He was very lucky that was ALL that broke!

One place on the floor bent dangerously down if you stepped near it. We told the pilot about it when he came back after three days bringing in more gas. He said, "Ya, hey. I know, don't step there. What the hell, it's not the Waldorf." Then he flew away. (The procedure in the fly-in camps if the fishermen notice anything that needs repair, is to tell the pilot. He either fixes the small stuff, if he has time, or he is supposed to report it for repairs back at the main base.)

There was a huge, boarded up hole on the outside wall that they told us, a black bear came through one day. They said that two fishermen were sleeping in the upper bunks when it ripped the plywood off and came in. They were petrified, and didn't move! The bear ate their loaves of bread and cookies that were on the table. It then left through a screened window. The outfitter told us that a bear would always leave by a different way than the one it came in.

There were two lower bunks and two upper bunks. After hearing that story, there was no trouble getting two guys to climb up and take those top bunks.

We were talking about that story when we went to bed on the second night. We were all in our sleeping bags except Bill. He turned the air knob tight on the Coleman lantern for the night then beat it into his sleeping bag before the light went off. Anyone, who has ever used a Coleman light, knows you have about one minute of light after you turn that knob and reach total darkness.

Total darkness was the word for it. No stars, no street lights, car lights, nothing ……. It was DARK! After about a half-hour, we could hear thumping on an outside wall. It would stop and start again in about a minute. Remember the bear story and how dark I explained it was. Add to that, a little imagination.

Bill and Dan, the two guys in the lower bunks, began to shine their flashlights everywhere. I was in a top bunk so I felt somewhat more comfortable than, I'm sure, they did. After all, I was close to the rafters and could jump up there if I had to. Up there, it would be just me and the mice.

The thumping started up again and seemed to shake one whole side of that flimsy-built plywood camp. Dan and Bill seemed to jump up at the same time and they moved the table and chairs against the door. The door had no lock. I think that a very strong wind could have blown it open. They piled our coolers, the table, chairs, tackle boxes, anything that they could find loose, against that door.

Then Dave started to tease them. "Go back to sleep you guys. Don't be so afraid of the wildlife. Look at Bob and I. We stayed in our bunks." And, it sounded like he was holding back from laughing as he was talking. You couldn't see in the total darkness. He was just a voice coming from a dark upper bunk.

The "bottom two," couldn't go back to sleep if they wanted to. They were saying, 'What if it ……," and "If it comes through there ……." Dave (top bunk) then, couldn't hold it back any longer. He laughed until you could hear him crying. He said, "That was me pounding on this outside wall." I could hear Dan say, "Let's put his sleeping bag on a lower bunk when he's out fishing tomorrow."

There was dew covering both windows in the camp at sun-up. We looked out at the lake and it appeared like smoke was rising slowly off of the lake's surface. That's what they call, Canadian Mist. It's a beautiful sight. All of this made the thin camp cold. We made a fire in the tin heater. Paper plates, fish grease, paper towels, and not much of anything else filled the stove for heat.

The stove turned cherry-red in no time at all. Then the stovepipe started to go, "Woof, Woof, Woof!" It was like it built up pressure, then exploded. We probably blew a chipmunk nest out of the stovepipe.

We finally convinced ourselves that those bear stories were probably just that, stories.

The outfitter even seemed to make improvements. He flew in two "Good ole boys" that he found somewhere to make minor repairs to the camp on our third day there. The first thing that they did was to crawl up onto the roof to fix any leaks. We told them about the chipmunk holes on each gable end. They promptly fixed that by wedging a bar of soap into each end. They said that the chipmunks wouldn't eat the soap so they wouldn't come in. Dave said to me, "Don't bet on it. Those chipmunks will probably take that soap down to the lake and clean themselves up."

Then we told them about the hole in the roof near the front wall. One of them saw the hole and poured a whole can of tar around and down the hole. The tar leaked down the inside wall and onto a 6-volt flashlight that we had sitting on a shelf there. It took Vic the better part of a morning to clean off all of that tar from the flashlight.

They then explained to us that the plane was coming back just before dark to take them out. Their pay was that if they finished repairs early, they could fish the lake for a few hours. Their looking for needed repairs was over. The tall, skinny one said, "I think that we're done. Do you have any tie?" (Canadian pronunciation for tea).

We gave them a cup of coffee and we quickly went fishing. I'll say this for them, they were better fishermen than they were repairmen. They had their poles, nightcrawlers, and a black plastic garbage bag. When they came back in, they had some nice 16-inch trout in that plastic garbage bag.

While they were waiting on the shore for the plane, one looked at the camp and said, "What the hey, it don't look too bad. You've got to remember, it's not the Waldorf."

After that, our saying up there became, "What the hey, it's not the Waldorf!"

The outhouse was up on a hill to the right of the camp. You didn't have to be modest and shut the door because one whole wall was missing. It was lying on the ground.

The fourth night, we all woke up to a "Clap, Clap, Clap, Clap," sound of something strange running through the kitchen/living room area. Bill shined his flashlight and we saw a mouse running. He had his tail caught in a mousetrap that we set and was dragging it behind him. The more noise that trap made as it bounced behind him, the faster he seemed to run. It must have scared him, too. Finally, he ran outside through a mouse hole. The trap was too big for the hole so it came off and stayed inside.

One consolation, the fishing for speckled trout, (brookies) was excellent. We were well ready to leave though, on our pick-up day. We had all of our gear packed and piled out on the landing, waiting for the plane.

When the plane touched down and taxied to the dock and stopped, the pilot loaded noticeably fast and kept looking over his shoulder. We were wondering why he was in such a hurry. The flying weather looked good. So we asked him. "The last time that I loaded out of this lake, a big, black bear chased me and that fishing party into the plane. We had to wait until it left so we could finish loading."

We all looked back at the shore and, I think, we may have set some kind of record with loading that plane.

Grr.

CHAPTER 17

THE DAY THE WOLF ALMOST GOT JOE

We were stream fishing for trout this hot, August, afternoon in the Newberry area. There were three of us, Joe, Bill, and I. There weren't many mosquitoes but the horseflies were big and pesty. They like to bite the top of your ears and will take a piece of meat out like a Mike Tyson bite.

Joe was a short guy who loved to trout fish. He wore waders that reached just under his chin. He had one major fault. He was afraid of most anything he couldn't see and snakes that he could see.

The stream water was warm. It was hot wearing hip boots so I could imagine how Joe felt in those waders. He was the only one I knew who fished with waders at that time. They probably gave him an extra foot of water protection because of his shorter legs.

He had a way of always "shadowing" you on the stream when you fished. He'd wait and see if you got a bite, then he would ease in on your fishing spot from the other side of the creek bank, just like it was natural. Joe and I went upstream and Bill was a long way downstream.

Bill always had a habit of making some kind of noise when he fished alone, like, singing, hooting like an owl, or whatever. He and I fished together a lot and I didn't think much about it as I always could tell where he was.

This day, all was quiet where I was fishing except for the stream gurgling by and Joe always pressing to catch the fish I'd get biting first. It didn't do any good to tell Joe to back off because he'd have an answer like, "No, that's one of my favorite spots and I think I was there first." He was scaring more fish than either one of us were catching because he felt he had some God-given duty to step in the stream ever so often to reach out farther. I could take a trout survey by watching those brookies dash a stream-bend ahead of him.

As we gradually fished farther upstream, the water became deeper. Some holes appeared deeper than Joe's waders did so he'd climb onto the opposite bank and would fish across from me.

He looked sideways once, and saw a huge pine snake slowly coming down the stream bank by him. I swear he jumped a foot higher out of those waders. You could see his neck and chest for that second before he settled back into them. Joe looked again at the snake and the snake looked at him. Joe then took off through the brush upstream crashing around like a startled buck. I came around the next bend and there was Joe standing out on a sandbar re-stringing his line.

The water was really deep here so he couldn't cross but he waited for me and then began fishing near my line again. This again was normal fishing procedure for Joe. I think he felt that if he left you alone, you'd catch more fish than him. This way, even if no one caught anything, he was satisfied that he wasn't second best.

The water was deep now and Joe knew there was a big pine snake downstream from him. He had no intention of ever going back downstream. The sun was now going down and long shadows were forming as the sun was fading. All at once, we heard the most mournful howl off in a distance downstream. Joe's eyes showed noticeable fear. Then we heard it again! This time, it sounded much closer… Joe said, "What the hell was that?!" I figured, this might get him out of my fishing hole as we were now almost crossing lines.

Trying to sound a little excited, I said, "It sure sounds like a timber wolf … you know, the DNR planted some up here. They probably ate all the deer around here and are now looking for something else." Joe didn't say anything. He just kept looking out of the corner of his eyes behind him.

Then we heard that terrible, mournful howl again!! MUCH MUCH closer and this time you could hear brush crackling! You knew SOMETHING was coming…. I said, "Your not afraid, are you Joe?" He said, "Hell, no!" He thought for a while, then said, "A wolf is afraid of a man, aren't they?" I said, "Normally, yes, but if they have no deer to eat … you know, Joe, you're about the size of a deer and it could be hungry."

The wolf cry came again, much closer. I figured about three creek bends back. Joe hunkered down in his waders. All you could see of his face was his eyes on up, looking like he was thinking hard. He wanted to jump somewhere but didn't know where to jump.

Minutes later, that low pitiful, hungry-sounding wolf cry started again with brush crackling loudly about two creek bends behind us. Joe made his decision. If that wolf got him, it wouldn't get him easily. He jumped into the stream with his waders. The water appeared to be about a foot over his head. The creek was about 15 feet across. All I could see of Joe was the top of his head and a mud cloud from him running on the creek bottom to get across. (Yes, you can run across a creek bottom if you have waders on full of water to hold you down and you are determined enough.) Joe did it. He came up on my side and I helped him pour the water out of his waders. I said, "Why did you ever do that?" He said, "Look, that wolf was on my side of the creek. (He felt safer by me.) The next time a wolf comes up on your side, I'll carry YOUR hip boots home."

Just then, Bill came into sight and said, "Hey, how'd you guys like my wolf call?" Joe looked at him in disbelief then … if looks could have killed…! When I told Bill the story, he laughed until he had to sit down. Joe just glared at him. He seemed relieved in one way, but still upset in another. We all thought this was a good time to head for the car and call it a day.

Bill and I laughed almost all the way home as we re-ran the detail of Joe's wolf. Poor Joe said, "It COULD have been a wolf." We said, "It sure sounded like a wolf. Anyone would have done what you did, Joe."

Ya, Sure ……

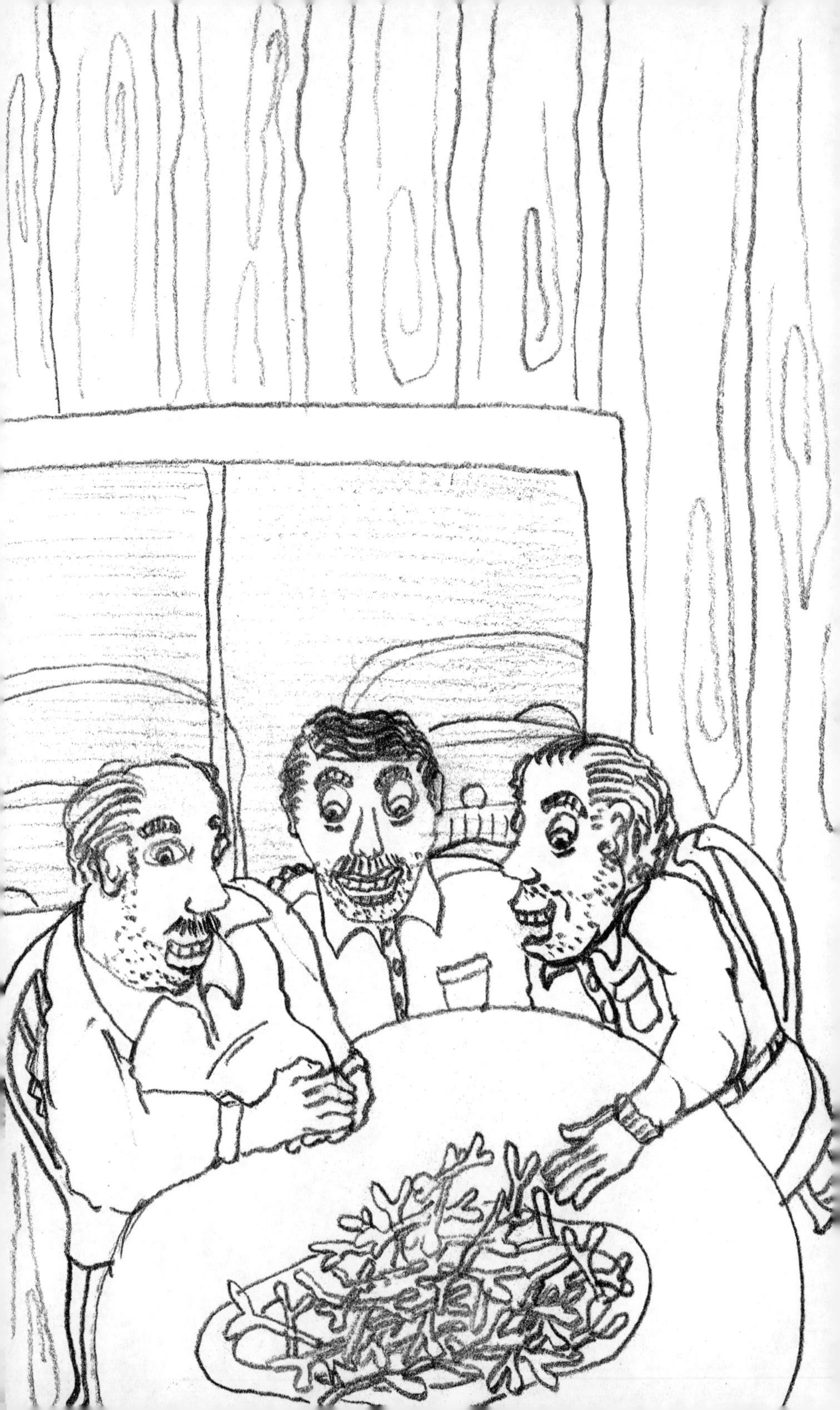

CHAPTER 18

TROUT STREAM FISHING WITH THE WOOD TICKS

I don't know of anyone who likes wood ticks. The first few, warm days of spring seems to bring them out in full force. Grassy areas, hardwoods, and swamps seem to be their favorite living places. (That doesn't leave a whole lot of other areas to go into.) They also will go into the softwoods but not as many as you will find in the hardwoods.

During the trout stream-fishing season, they always are at their peak. The best trout streams always seem to go through cedar swamps. You know you are going to get full of the little critters before you go in there.

You have to be a dedicated trout fisherman to intentionally put up with the feeling of having them crawl all over on you. And then running the chance of having one bore into you and possibly cause an infection, and after you pick off the first one, have that feeling that they are crawling all over you.

We like the thrill of catching brook trout under logs and in small pools in these streams. That's the only logic that I can tell you, why we wade into these wood tick ripe, areas. There was no spray or lotion to help keep them off of you. We could repel the mosquitoes but not those silent, lurking ticks.

We'd catch a fish, pick off a few noticeable ticks, and continue fishing. The only way that we found to live with them, is to try to ignore them, pick them off, don't let it bother you, and go on with whatever your doing.

Ben and I were fishing on Kelly Creek (Menominee County) one particular day. We fished for the afternoon until it reached the point where you could still safely see to come back out of the swamp before dark.

Two friends of ours fished that same area the week before. They stayed in the woods too late! They couldn't see well enough to keep onto a pathway out of there. The only way out for them, was to get into the stream and walk in the stream all the way out. That cedar swamp was too thick to attempt anything else but that.

The stream has windfalls about every 20-30 feet across that you had to climb or step over. Their walk out in the daylight would have taken them approximately, an hour. By climbing over all of these obstacles, they said it took them three hours to find the road and their car.

They came out full of bruises from slipping, falling over the windfalls, and being slapped in the face by limbs that they couldn't see in the dark.

After Ben and I fished, we picked off as many ticks as we could find. You never seem to find them all on the first "Look-over." We were hot, tired, sweaty, feeling "crawly" and very hungry. We saw a restaurant on the way home that advertised "Homestyle chicken, all you can eat, for $6.95."

The price was a deal, if the chicken was any good. The restaurant had tables and booths. We took a booth figuring that if anything were still crawling on us, we wouldn't draw attention from the other customers. They had such high backs to the booths, that a person had to be right in front of it to see if anyone was in there.

The owner appeared to be a real friendly person. He had on a white shirt (looked a little out of place in the part of the county where we were) and a big cigar in his mouth. His head was as round as a pumpkin. Bill picked off the first wood tick since we came in and put it in his water glass. It was swimming and struggling around in there when the waitress came over to take our order. You could see her eyes fix onto that glass, but she didn't say anything. Pretty soon, we had two more ticks in that glass.

She came back with the chicken and again stared at that wood tick glass. We hadn't eaten anything worth mentioning since breakfast, so, we were in the mood for that "All you can eat" business.

After the first plateful of ½ chicken each, we filled another equal plate. The manager came around, smiling, and said, "How's the chicken, guys? Enjoy ….. Eat all you can." Ben looked at him, very sober like, and promised that we would…..

After that plateful, he came by again. I noticed that he wasn't smiling as much at us now, but was looking at the pile of bones that we had. "Help yourself, boys," he said with a weak smile. We went back for a third time. We

were hungry and it tasted good. He came around again, looked at our bigger pile of chicken bones, rolled his eyes and never said a word. He just left.
The waitress came back again, with the usual, "Is everything all right?" She said, "You must have been out fishing and got full of ticks. I don't feel so bad now. I thought that first tick in your glass might have been in there when I gave it to you." (She was one up on us...).

I could hear the owner working the cash register and saying, "Come back again," "Don't be a stranger," "Thank you." When we paid our bill, I noticed that he looked over his shoulder into our booth at the pile of chicken bones. He gave us our change, smiled weakly, and that was it. He probably was thinking of changing that, "All you can eat" sign.

Those wood ticks are no joke. A lot of fishermen would never go into a cedar swamp to fish a stream like we did during the tick season. I saw one fisherman on another trip in this area, hallucinating in his parked car. I first thought he was having a heart attack or a seizure. He would fade from conscious to unconscious and back again. He said that he just seen to many wood ticks.

They were really thick where he was parked. You could literally see them crawling around on the ground. We gave him a drink of water, rolled down his windows for him and it didn't take long and we saw him leave.

Jokin-Joes....There is always someone with a good sense of humor wherever there is hardship. Jokin-Joe could laugh at anything. He owned a bar in the middle of this "tick" population. It was called, you probably guessed it,

"Jokin-Joes." Joe lived with all of these ticks for so long that he seemed to feel, why fight them?

Most all of the trout fishermen that fished in this area would stop at Jokin-Joes after they were done fishing. It was one place where you could relax out of the ticks. We stopped there after one of these trips. There were three strangers sitting at the bar. They looked frightened, like, they took all they could of those wood ticks.

Joe was working on them now. The middle guy didn't seem to be the brightest light in the harbor. Joe said, "You think that you saw a lot of ticks? We had a guy in here a few weeks ago that even had his whole car covered with them. I don't know where he went, but he sure took a lot of them home with him."

When those guys left, they went out and checked over their car…. twice!

A local resident living in this good trout country told me that the ticks are real survivors. He is an excellent fisherman and a marginal farmer. He said, "One day, I was walking back home following the cows. I noticed the tick's just "rain" down from a tree onto a cow's back as it passed under that tree. They can sense the presence of an animal by its body heat." If you believe that, we don't have much of a chance to avoid them.

He also said, "Those ticks do seem to serve some function. They keep a lot of people out of the woods when the animals are having their young." By stretching it a bit, that may be one value of wood ticks.

CHAPTER 19

AN UNFORGETTABLE CHARACTER ITALIAN LEONARD

He was a neighbor of my father-in law's on the "north side" of Iron Mountain. It seemed like most of the Italians lived on the north side with a few "Cousin Jacks" mixed in.

He was a true pioneer like some that can be found in any community. He knew how to do things "where there were never any directions written down." "Farming" a whole city lot next to his house was his full-time hobby and work for the years that I knew him.

Tomatoes, LOTS of tomatoes, seemed to be his main crop. They were tied to five-six foot high poles rather than normal tomato stakes. No one knew how he could get those tomato plants to grow so fruitful and tall. He was always mixing up some type of home remedy fertilizer. We knew that rabbit manure was one main ingredient.

He'd pick bushels of tomatoes and cook them down to paste on a wood stove in his back porch. He'd do this night and day similar to someone else cooking down maple syrup. One day, he told me that he discovered a neighbor who lived a block away, was stealing his tomatoes. This neighbor would open his shirt and fill it up with forty or fifty tomatoes and go back home.

Leonard said, "Come-a here, my-a friend." He said that the neighbor looked startled but came over and Leonard then gave him a big hug (an Italian custom with friends). "I-a squeezed him-a so hard-a that all of those-a tomatoes popped open and the guy-a looked like-a he was-a bleeding to death-a." That was the last time that he took any tomatoes.

He made his tomato paste in pint fruit jars. Most everything that Leonard made was with pint fruit jars. If you drank his wine, it was from a pint fruit jar. He had a "walk-in" basement with a sand floor. The sand floor was by choice. One half of it was a wine cellar. It was dark down there and I guessed that the sand floor must have had something to do with keeping his wine at a certain temperature.

Leonard made a lot of different kinds of Italian wines. One thing about them, they were all excellent! He'd invite me to go downstairs every time that he'd see me at my father-in-law's house, next door. Of course, this invitation was to sample his wines. To an Italian wine maker, selling some of their wine for a money profit wasn't all that important. Honest praise after drinking a jar, now, that was what it was all about.

He'd turn a small, wooden spigot from a wooden, wine barrel and give you a pint jar to taste and evaluate. A pint of wine is a lot of wine. If you didn't drink it all after it was given to you, it could be looked at as an insult or disrespect toward the wine and wine maker. I learned some tasting pointers from my Italian father-in-law.

"Now, this one has a fine body to it and an excellent color." He'd smile and say "Try-a this-a one…" I'd drink and say, "Good texture, dry, but not too dry…etc, etc." "Try-a this-a one."

He'd sit at the little wooden table that he had down there, and taste a matching pint along with you. This one time, after we were "sampling," he looked up at the ceiling and said, 'This-a one is-a good pint-a wine, Boss. It-a has-a good-a body and a good-a alcohol. It's-a no cheap-a wine, Boss. I-a could-a give-a you some-a for a little bit. You-a couldn't-a go-a wrong." It appeared very much like he had his share of wine and was trying, in the biggest way, to make a deal selling some to the Lord. Leonard was very religious.

He could graft any fruit tree successfully and have many different varieties of that fruit grow on the same tree. All of his wines weren't made from grapes. His apple trees had at least three to four varieties of apples growing on each one from his skillful grafting. The tree limbs would have so many apples that he would place clothesline poles under them to prevent them from breaking to the ground.

My father-in-law would say, "Leonard could probably get apples to grow on a maple tree…well, …almost."

He wasn't a hunter but if he spotted a rabbit in his garden, the next day he had rabbit, Polenta, and red sauce. I think if a cat came into his garden, he would have had Polenta, red sauce, and mystery meat.

Leonard raised rabbits to eat, in some little coops by his backyard shed. He said, "They-a have-a good life. All-a they do-a is eat and breed. This-a big one is-a always smiling."

Everyone should be as content and peaceful as Leonard. He told me, "Rabbits, Polenta, Red sauce, and-a few pints of-a good-a wine." "Oh, and-a you-a can't forget-a the wife. You-a have to-a give her-a some too." Then he laughed............

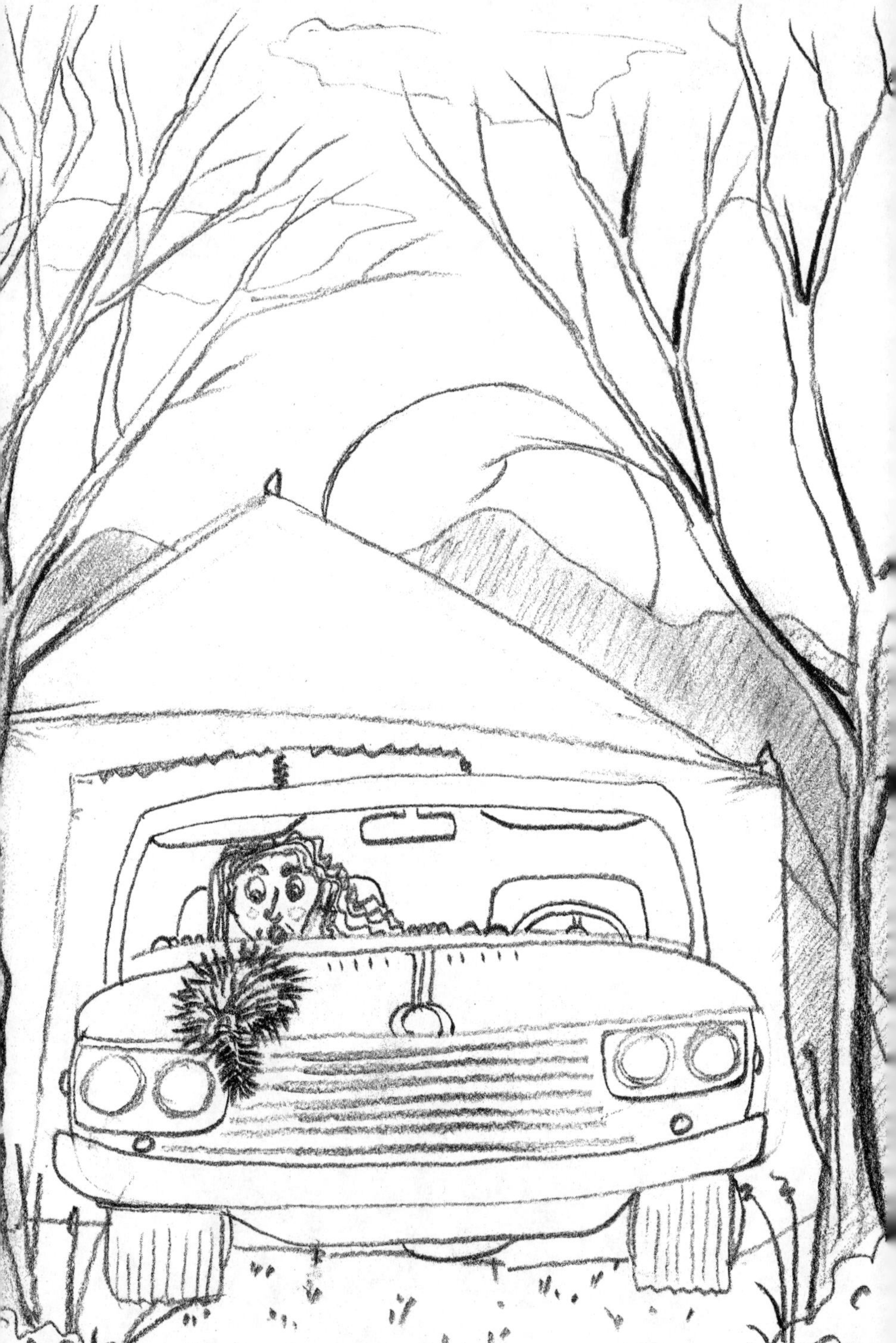

CHAPTER 20

THE SUSPICIOUS FISHERMAN'S WIFE

Ben and I are fishing buddies. At times, we'd go on day trips or overnighters. We always came home with fish, a cheerful attitude, and some good stories. One could conclude that we always had a great time.

Now, Ben's wife was somewhat suspicious by nature. She thought he was having TOO good of a time. After all, he didn't seem that happy at home before he left. She felt that it was her solemn duty to keep her husband nervous and on his toes …. keep verbally jabbing him. She felt that no husband should be that relaxed and happy.

Her job, as a beautician, kept her in steady conversation with other women who talked over …. who knows what? She seemed to feel that she was missing out on something. Our next planned fishing trip was to be an overnighter up near Channing. We were going to fish the Ford River. Being that we were there before, we knew where we could catch some nice brook trout.

Ben called me the day before the trip and informed me that his wife was going along with us on this trip. I asked, "Why?" He said, "Because it's nice to have your wife on a fishing trip with you." I knew right there that his wife had to be standing right next to him, probably to check my response.

I said, "Happy to have her, Ben, but it doesn't seem like the kind of trip that she'd enjoy." As a beautician, her hair and make-up was always perfect. Also, a perfect manicure and she probably would want to wash up with soap, too (we were normally pretty well covered with mosquito spray until we would go home).

At first glance the next day, I was wondering if she was going to a different place than we were. I knew how the conditions were where we were going. If she was coming with us, well, she just didn't look right.....

We drove up to that area and set up our two-cot tent somewhere in the middle of the night, using the car headlights to see. The wall tent fit two cots and an isle. Ben's wife said she'd sleep in the front seat of the car (I was thinking, good luck with those seatbelts). We were dead tired from working and from the drive. I laid down and fell asleep fast. I learned long ago, whoever falls asleep first, hears no snoring.

Suddenly, we were awaken by a flashing light reflecting through the walls of the tent. It was getting brighter and brighter. Then ...... you could hear a train engine coming closer flashing that light. It was getting brighter, brighter, closer, and closer.... We both jumped up in a panic and felt for railroad tracks through the tent floor. Then we shined our flashlight in front of the car. Just as that train got within 50 yards of us, it made a sweeping turn with the tracks and passed by. What a feeling!

Then, sometime during the night, a porcupine climbed onto the car's hood and rested up against the windshield. Ben's wife woke up with the sunlight, sat up on the seat, looked out of the windshield and that porky was looking back at her about a foot away from her face. She screamed loud enough to be heard a mile away. That porky just sat there and looked at her. Ben had to chase it away with a stick.

She calmed down and said that she'd fry the eggs and bacon for breakfast. Something didn't look right with her. Her hair was flat against one side of her head from sleeping in the car. Ben said, "For God's sake, don't tell her. She has no mirror here and won't know about it."

We just smiled and it DID look unusual. A full, fluffed-out head of hair on one side and the other side flat against her head.

The campfire smoke was now starting to swirl her way and completely covered her with smoke for what seemed to be, a minute. She was coughing and complaining, "Do something about this smoke!" Ben smiled at me and said, "Why is it when men are dirty they look manly. When women get dirty, they just look dirty?" Ben's wife was still groping with herself, trying to figure out where we got all of that enjoyment from these fishing trips.

After the breakfast, we poured the frying pan's bacon grease onto a rock, for no particular reason. Well, after that breakfast ordeal, we fixed up our fishing poles and divided up the worms. She said, "Don't think I'm going to bait that hook Ben, you'll have to fish close to me so you can do that." He looked at her, smiled, and looked away. I thought right there, Ben's high enjoyment from these trips included being apart from his wife for awhile. Like, absence makes the heart grow fonder?

We found that we were camped about a half a city block from the Ford River, not bad for setting up camp in the dark. As we were walking toward the river, in single file, she was saying, "I better not see a pine snake! Why do we have to walk so far? We're skipping a lot of water right here!"

We started fishing. After a minute, she said, "If they don't bite soon, I'm going back to the car ... and Ben, you have to come back too. I don't want to be here alone!" He looked at her, then at me, and I thought if the water was deeper, it looked like he'd have pushed her in.

Ben and I caught about 5 brookies up til then. The mosquitoes were now beginning to smell us and thought we were a nice "City lunch." His wife, Fay, swatted at mosquitoes, and said, "I don't know why you think this is fun. We could have bought a nice fish fry and went to the Casino. Nooo, you had to come out here." She kept it up. "If this is such a good sport, don't you think you'd see more people out here doing this?"

"Whoever told you that this was a good fishing spot?" Ben then said to me, "Let's walk up to the beaver pond." Do you realize that's about a mile upstream?" I said. "It's not that bad," answered Ben. I think that he wanted to lose her in the woods or exhaust all of her talking strength.

We caught a few more fish and I think Ben was looking for a pine snake in the worst way. Fay then said, "I'm not walking any farther. I'll wait here for you." "Stay

close, honey" he said, "so the bears don't get you. I've seen some bear signs but didn't want to alarm you." Fay, one step behind Ben said, "Why won't the bears get us anyway if we're bunched up?"
Ben smiled, "Bears are slow thinkers. They probably couldn't decide whom to eat first. By the time they go, 'eeny, meeny, miney, mo' a few times, we can walk away from them." He looked back at me and shook his head. He softly said, "God, she'll believe anything."

We had 14 nice trout by noon and decided to go fry them up for lunch. Fay was still agreeable to cook lunch. The fire smoke was again curling around with the wind. By now, she figured out how to back up and avoid most of it.

She said to Ben who was cleaning the fish, "How do I know when the fish are done?" He told her, "Fry them until their eyes pop out. Then they're done." "If you think I'm going to fry fish with they're heads on in this frying pan and watch they're eyes pop out, your crazy!" She told him, "Cut those heads off."

I was looking at her. Her hair was smashed down flat against her head on one side, her face was all dirty from wood smoke, and it was the first time I ever saw her fingernails dirty. Like Ben said, "It's a good thing that she doesn't have a mirror."

Before Fay dished up the lunch, she said, "You two should go wash up before you eat. You look a mess." We smiled and thought again, it's a good thing she doesn't have a mirror or we'd be on our way home by now.

All was quiet that night as we turned in. About an hour later, we heard, "Crunch, crunch, crunch." It sounded like someone was working a big file on a steel bar. We turned on the flashlight, and checked in the direction of that sound. There was a porcupine literally scraping his teeth on that rock where we poured the grease. He wanted that grease and was trying to chew it off.

Ben thought a few well-thrown rocks would be better than having his wife scream at it. We chased it away before she could hear the noise from inside the car.

The next morning, the sunrise was beautiful. The birds were singing, and we, again, went to the river to fish. We left Fay by a normally good fishing spot. It was a 10-foot round culvert extending out about 12 feet from the road. She sat on the very end of it fishing downstream. She was sitting there for only about 20 minutes and a skunk walked down the road not more than 20 feet away from her.

There she was. Sitting a good 20 feet from any solid ground, fast moving water below her into a deep pool and no where to go. "Ben, …. Oh Ben, …. Softly she was calling. Ben smiled at me and said, "That's the quietest that I ever heard her call me since we were married." The skunk finally just walked away.

No more of that spot for her! She made us agree to fish for only two more hours and then quit. This time though, she came with us along the stream bank. She no more than got ready to fish and she slipped on the muddy clay riverbank and fell in …. "That's it! That's it! Everybody back to the car!!"

Ben never seemed to argue with her and immediately started back to the car. I looked at her steaming toward the car. She looked like someone that fell headfirst down a muddy stream bank. She was a sight to behold. She stared straight ahead, mad-like, and said, "So you guys call this fun!"

As we were driving home, Ben said, seriously, "So what casino would you like to stop at, Honey?"

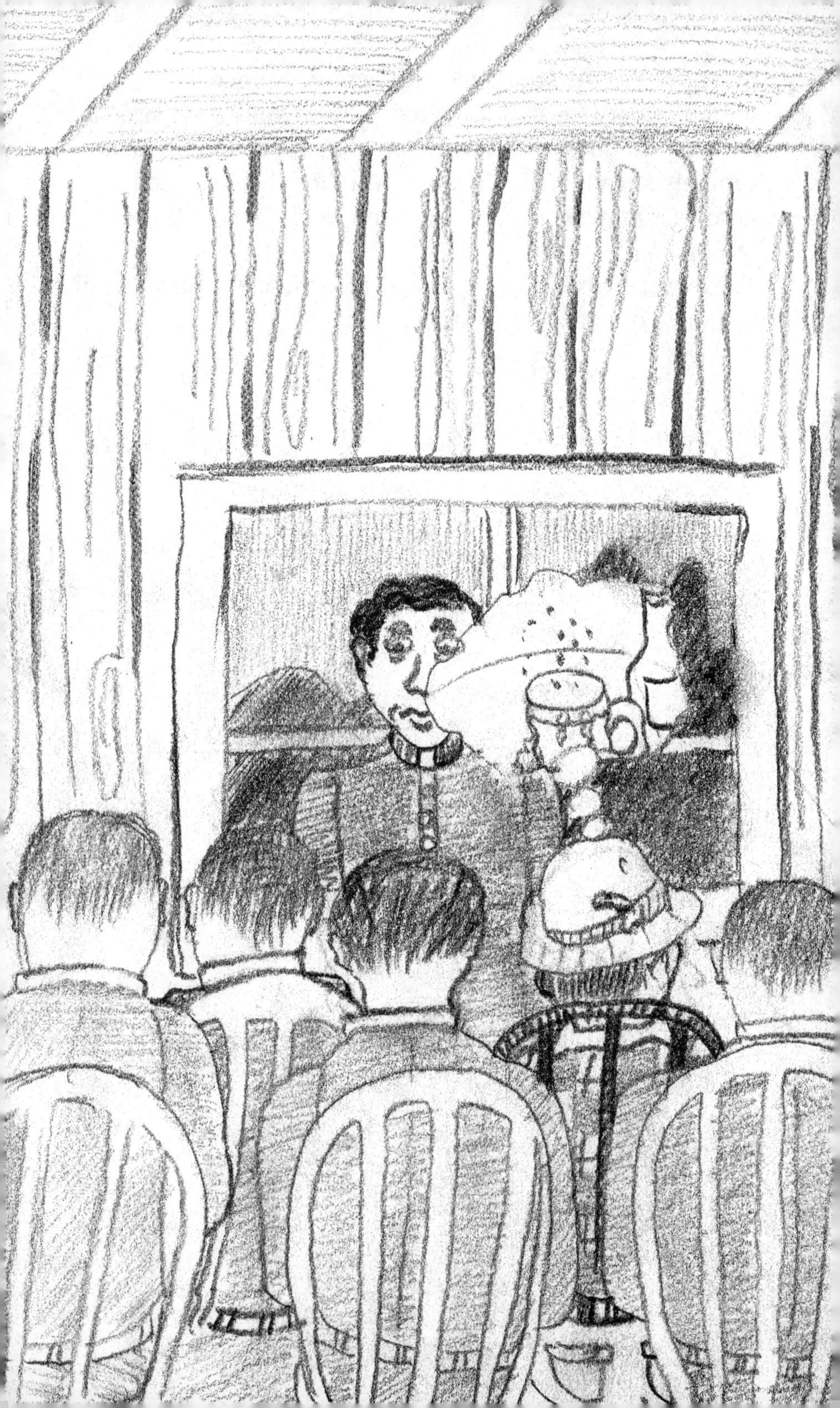

CHAPTER 21

PLANNING A FLY-IN FISHING TRIP
(SOME TRIPS FLY, SOME DON'T)

Sounds easy, right? Wrong. Vic (a partner in my fishing trips) was invited to go on another Canadian weeklong fishing trip this June. Somehow, he volunteered or was asked to plan and buy the week's groceries to take with. After all, he had experience planning the meals out from many trips before.

Ed and his three sons made up the rest of the party. Ed told Vic to "buy what we need" and we'll split the cost. He happily drove 30 miles to a larger food store and bought soda on sale at $2.00 a 12 pack. Four 12 packs. When he got home, he told Ed of his good price find. Ed told him, "We'll have to drink that ourselves because the kids (age 30,27,25) don't drink any carbonated products."

Vic, who is a champion when it comes to drinking beer or booze, immediately asked him if they drink either of those. Ed told him, "I'm afraid not. They don't drink alcohol either." Right about now, Vic was at an all-time low. He could go without most groceries but not without booze on a fishing trip.

Vic said, "What if one of them gets bit by a snake?" Ed told him, "They'd have to suck out the poison." Vic asked, "What if one of them breaks a leg?" Ed said, "We'll have to splint it and give him aspirin." Vic countered in desperation, "What if one of them dies?" Ed said, "What, you'd want to drink to that too?"

"By the way," Ed said, "We all have to send up $100.00 for deposit money now to reserve our trip and cabin." Vic reluctantly gave his $100.00 for deposit. He then went back to the store and bought 4 cans of pork and beans and 4 cans of corn. He was pleased with himself on the way home because of the cheap prices he got and well, everyone must eat beans and corn.

He called Ed again and told him of his good purchases. Ed said, "Well, you and I will have to eat that because the boys don't eat pork and beans and above all, they don't like corn." Vic then did what he should have long ago, asked what they DO eat? "They will eat most anything else but no tomato products, canned meat, white bread, sausage, and no sweets. Feel free to buy anything but that."

He thought, what do these guys REALLY eat? Then it flashed in his mind, STEAK? EXPENSIVE STEAK? Vic already had his deposit money committed and couldn't get it back. What a problem! He was starting to roll with this one.

The next weekend, they all got together to meet each other. He looked them over and they looked like they all had money and didn't mind spending it. He started thinking how did I get into this? Ed introduced everyone and told Vic that his one son, "Sleepy Joe" would ride in Vic's new truck with him. "He'll keep you company but you have to watch him if he drives. He has a tendency to fall asleep when he's driving."

Vic started to think of all of those deep drop-offs on those Canadian highways and knew he couldn't go to sleep if this guy relieved him. Ed suggested that Vic take "Sleepy Joe" over to the local bar and get better acquainted for the trip. Now that sounded good to Vic. He promptly ordered a Brandy and white soda and told "Sleepy Joe" that he was buying. Sleepy smiled at him and ordered a glass of water. Vic said he watched him drinking that water and could feel himself getting sick.

When they got back together, Ed began to tell them what he knew about the cabin. He said, "And now about the bunks," Vic interrupted him and said, "Hold it, Hold it!" (He was thinking that he would have to over-pay on the groceries, couldn't drink in comfort, had to stay awake even for the relief driver, he was at least going to get a bottom bunk.) "I got this bad back and these kids are all younger than me. I want a bottom bunk."

Ed looked at him, curiously, and said, "I was about to say that the cabin is large. Everyone will have a bottom bunk. There is also a huge main lodge that is already reserved and filled by two groups. One group is Baptist ministers and the other group is doctors. They were good enough to ask us what group we'd like to socialize with and be their guests. I took the liberty to tell them that we'd be happy with the ministers because the boys don't drink and those doctors are known to really booze it up on vacation." Vic looked back at him like a puppy that had its mother being taken away from him.

They finally got to the lake and the cabin. Vic (being out of his normal element) quietly went along with the social conditions and listening to the ministers. Then one day after the main lodge visit, Vic said, "I'm going for a swim."

Ed said, "He did pretty good too. He ran across the top of the water for about 8 feet before he sank in." He asked, "Vic, you swim good with your clothes on. Why didn't you take them off?" And, Vic looked back at him, kind of bewildered and said, "ALLELUIA!"

CHAPTER 22

TROUT FISHING WITH ROGER AND HIS NEW WIFE

This was Roger's first year of married life. It was a traumatic change for him. He assumed that because his wife was so agreeable with him BEFORE they got married that she'd blend right into his "woodsy" lifestyle as a natural thing. That was the first, big, wrong, assumption that he made.

Although I fished with him for a few years, I have to admit that his lifestyle was a bit different. I drove up to his camp in North-Menominee County one day. He wanted to go brook trout fishing in some of the small creeks that we knew of in the county.

Roger said with pride, "If we catch a nice meal of trout, my wife will cook them up for us. She's coming up from the city for supper."

We "paid our dues" with the mosquitoes and wood ticks as we were fishing those small streams until almost dark. We caught a limit each. Not too big, but we figured with fried potatoes, beans, and bread, we'd have a good, full meal.

As we drove back into his camp road, we saw that his new bride, Rosy, was already there. She came out of the camp with a big smile and asked if we caught any fish. Rog looked at me proudly, and said, "See, I'll bet she'd have even cleaned them for us."

Before we walked into the camp, she looked curiously at the new, G.I. cooking kettle that he had sitting on a stump in the yard. "What's that kettle doing outside?" she asked. Roger smiled, "I made spaghetti in it yesterday. I leave it out overnight and the raccoons lick off the hard-to-clean stuff. Then I take it inside and wash it." She looked at him and said, "I'm going home…"

He laughed quickly and said, "No, no, that was only a joke. Come on back in." Knowing Roger like I did, I knew that was standard procedure whenever he cleaned the spaghetti pot. He never liked to scrub the kettles and rarely joked.

His wife kind of wrinkled up her nose and put the frying pan on the stove as Roger salted and floured the fish. As they were frying, she said, "How do you know when these fish are done?" "Just like frying a hamburger, Honey." He said. She looked at him out of the corner of her eyes and said, "I'm going home." I guess she burned hamburgers too.

Roger, again, appeased her. "Hey, Holy Wah! I was only kidding. Just stay and cook." They tasted something like hamburgers, too.

After the meal, she said, "How did you get this camp so dirty?" Roger thought it was pretty well cleaned up. But, again, to appease, he said, "I was going to clean it up today before you came but we went out to catch some fresh fish for you."

"You didn't have to do that for me," she said. "I brought some TV dinners." Now, Roger hated TV dinners. He used to say (before he got married), "Anyone who eats TV dinners don't deserve a well-cooked, camp meal."

"Can't we go for a ride somewhere?" she said, "RIDE? It took two hours to get here." Roger muttered. Well, it finally got dark and we went to the two different bedrooms to sleep. The lights were out and all was settling down quietly in the camp.

Then I heard her say, "You expect ME to go to the toilet in that porcelain cookie jar?" I could hear Roger saying to her, "Please, Honey, don't ever put cookies in THERE!"

The next day she again said, "Don't you have any neighbors to visit up here?" Roger loved the solitude of the camp area. He relaxed here, listened to all of the different birds chirping, watched the chipmunks running around near the camp, and loved to see deer come to his bait pile that he would replenish just for that reason. "No neighbors? We can fix that… Let's have a big party up here next weekend. I'll invite all of my relatives," she said. "We'll have someone to visit with, anyway. A person could go buggy with all this quiet."

Roger hated her relatives about as much as he enjoyed going to his dentist. His dentist told him the last time, "Rog, if you start paying your bill, I'll use Novocain again." "Not that big uncle that you've got too?" "Yes, Uncle Al, too! He says that he's a very good fisherman.

You could learn something from him, you know. He's older than you." The only thing that Rog said he probably could learn from him was how to eat more and faster…

That uncle had a horse. Roger felt that the horse was smarter than the uncle was. When the uncle whipped the horse, the horse did tricks. He said, " If you whipped that uncle, all he would do is holler." So, Rog figured the horse was smarter than the uncle.

Roger pleaded with her, "Honey, I don't think that your Aunt Ann likes me." "I KNOW she don't," she replied. "You're going to have to change your ways. Lord knows, you couldn't expect HER to change." He said, quietly, to me, that he wished she'd change into a frog!

Rosy fried the fish, again, for our next lunch. "How do you like the fish?" she asked. "And if you complain, I'm going home." Rog looked up from his plate, closed one eye, rubbed his stomach, smiled through closed teeth and said, "Your getting a little better."

She took that as a compliment. Her mind seemed to be made up before anyone would answer her, anyway.

After the meal, she started swinging her head back and forth. Roger was looking at her and wondering, now what? "We'll have to make some changes up here to make this place more livable. You'll have to get rid of that bear rug. I don't like walking on dead animals. That border of empty shotgun shells that you have around the front room walls? Take them down, take them down. They are impossible to dust. It's funny that YOU never thought of these things, Roger."

Roger looked at me, smiled slowly, and then back at her. I thought to myself, you can't do it Rog, There are laws against that.

To throw her off pace, he said, "We're going to go fishing again, now, Dear." "O.K." she said, "Just don't bring back anymore of those slimy fish!" As we were fishing and after a long period of silence from Rog, he said, "She's very warm in bed, though, saves putting on an extra blanket." I thought, the poor guy was really straining to find something good. I'd have bought that extra blanket, anytime.

When I got back home, my wife said, "Have a good time, Honey? Let me reclean your fish so they're ready to cook when you freeze them." I smiled and thought how lucky "I" was. "How would you like to buy a new refrigerator or something?" I said. She looked back at me kind of suspiciously and said, "Come over here closer so I can smell your breath."

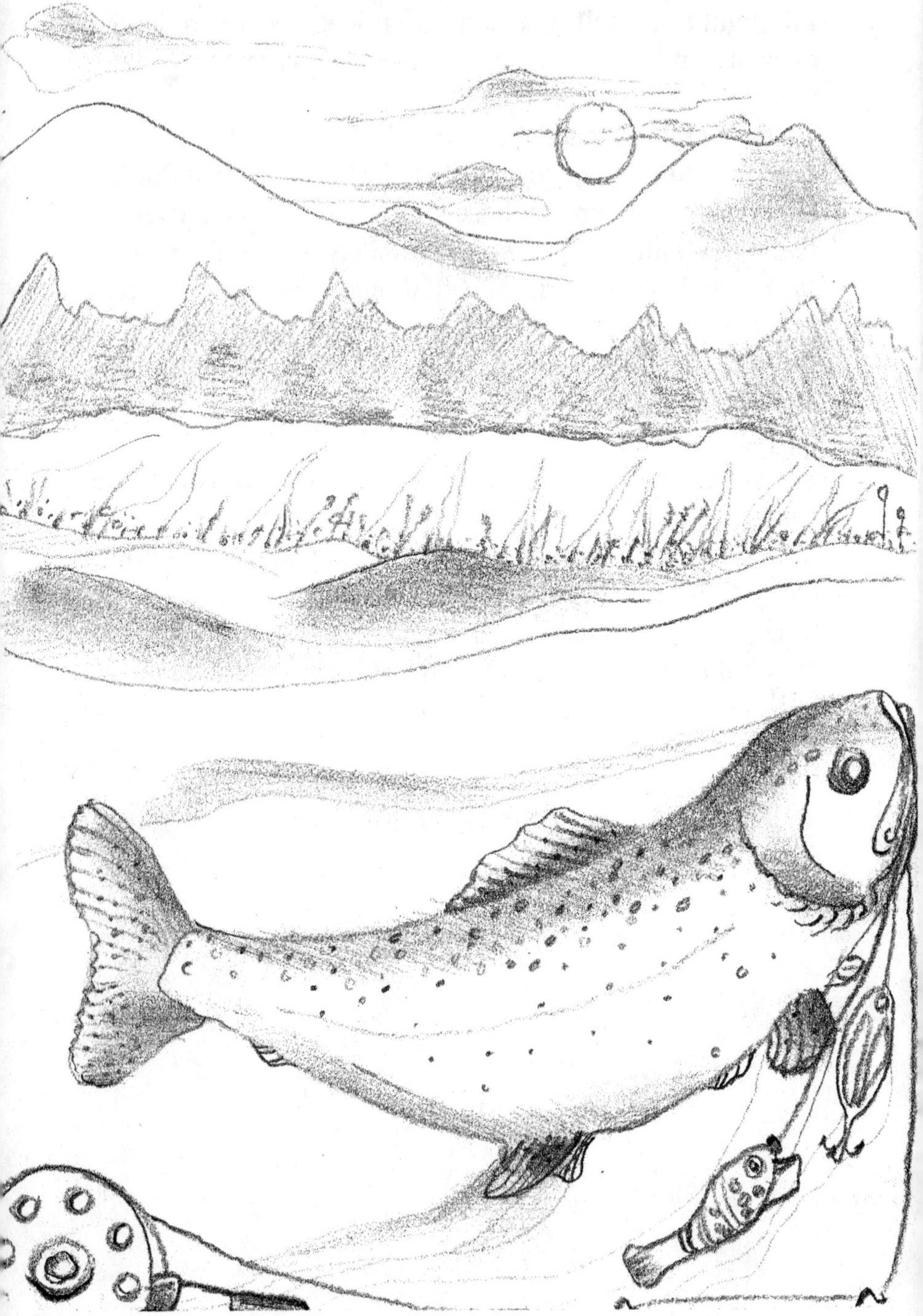

CHAPTER 23

SOME FAVORITE FISHING SPOTS

Everything needs some kind of identification or landmark to help find or explain where it is. Whether you live on 14th street or "two miles west of the Lost Lake Church," you gave directions to find you.

All seasoned fishermen have favorite names for their fishing spots. "Wright's Hole" is the first one that comes to my mind. It's been called that ever since I can remember. It's a wider place on the Pike River where you can look out and normally see, one to three larger brook trout finning their self watching upstream for their favorite food to wash down.

The only way to reach them is with a fly rod or spinning outfit. If you tell any of my fishing friends that you're going to "Wright's Hole," they know exactly where you're going and that you plan to fish.

Most good fishing locations that I know were named in honor of some person or a big fish that got away there.

BIG ANDY: Andy was one huge brook trout. We caught him a couple of times in a Canadian Lake. The Fly-in trout trips up there are still really worth it. That's getting to be one of the only ways to fish big trout. There are no roads to these lakes because of the impossible terrain. The rock outcrops are high and rugged. I would have died trying to walk out there. BIG ANDY broke a foot off of Bill's new Ultra-light spinning rod the first time that we missed him. The second time, he straightened out a fishhook after being on the line for at least 10 minutes. The third time, we had a fish pole leaning out on the side of the boat with a nightcrawler and split-shot sinker resting on the bottom of the lake. All at once, the pole banged against the side of the boat and started to be pulled overboard! We grabbed the pole and about the same time, BIG ANDY broke the surface water and threw the hook. We didn't have a chance to set the hook because of the slack line between the boat and that fish. How did we know it was the same fish each time? This lake has one particularly deep hole in the northwest corner. BIG ANDY must have declared it his own territory, as that's the spot we'd find him in.

BIG ANDY'S HOLE was the name thereafter, of that fishing spot. When anyone would go down to that end of the lake to fish, the other boat will always asked, "Did you fish BIG ANDY'S HOLE?" We guessed that he would weigh in at about 4-5 pounds.

We caught many smaller trout in that same spot, but never, yet, got BIG ANDY. That fishing spot is indeed, a deep hole. We marked it by lining up a tall, dead tree on one shore that has a large "bird hole" in it. We have seen wood ducks fly out of that hole. The opposite shore has a gravel bar projecting out into the water. We call that spot, MARY'S HOLE in honor of Mary who registers you and take's your money for the Fly-in trip.

The next year, the first spot everyone (we always go with a party of four fishermen) wanted to fish was "MARY'S HOLE". With a big smile, Bill said, "I'm going down to MARY'S HOLE and look for BIG ANDY."

No one thought that we'd see that fish again. There are other fishermen that also fish this lake, at times. Although, there is only a group of four fishermen allowed to fish it at one time. Normally, for a week. There is only one cabin on this entire lake. There are also many weeks when there are no fishermen on this lake.

Dave had one on there, last year, that kept moving around on the bottom after he hooked it. He was using an ultra-light spinning outfit with 4-pound test line. Normally, you can bring in a 10-pound trout with that setup, if you are careful.

There was no way that Dave could get that fish to rise up in the water so we could even get a look at it. He kept the line tight with the drag and the fish would take some line, give some back, but refused to come up. We were fishing in about 20 feet of water. You have to honor a fish like that to get a hole named for it. Finally, his hook straightened out and the fish got off. That had to be BIG ANDY or his brother.

The second day turned warmer and for some reason, the fish became more active. They were biting almost as fast as our split shot sinker would slowly go to the bottom. Then, WAM! Bill had one on that bent his pole almost in half! That pole never straightened out all the time that the fish was on.

It swam around the boat, under the boat, we pulled the motor up so it wouldn't tangle the line up, and then it swam away from the boat again. It had to be hooked good. It now was about 30 feet away from the boat and hardly pulling the line at all.

Bill reeled in slowly. It came in until it must have seen the boat and then it started to fight all over again. A few runs along side of the boat and we got it into the landing net. A beautiful, deep-red-bellied speckled trout! It had two other fish lines hanging out of its mouth. Those lines were extending about 6 inches out. He must have broken two lines before Bill tied into him. One line was almost dissolved but the other looked quite new yet.

FISH BOX RAPIDS: This was an easy one to name. We were fishing brook trout in the U.P.'s Huron Mountain area. We came to a good stretch of rapids where we caught almost a limit of trout. There were huge windfall trees across this stream. As I ducked under one large wind-wall, I reached up to steady my balance. Right where my hand rested on the top of that windfall, was a plastic fish-lure box "with all the fixings." New lures, spinners, split shot sinkers, leaders, and extra hooks. Someone could have forgotten it there as much as 2-3 years ago. There was moss covering part of it but everything inside of that box was like new. Thus, we named it, FISH BOX RAPIDS. Whenever we talk about catching fish in FISH BOX RAPIDS, we know, immediately, where we are talking about.

VIC'S SLOUGH: Vic got tangled around in there and wandered around for three or four hours before finding his way out. He's the only one that don't smile when we talk about fishing VIC'S SLOUGH.

MUSTANG SALLY'S: I never did hear how that spot got its name. I'll bet it was an interesting story, though.

TRAPPER'S POND: We found two, old, traps still wired to dead tree roots on the shore of this pond. Being that, there was an old beaver dam on the downstream end and a beaver house in the center, TRAPPER'S POND seemed to be a natural name for it.

THUNDER RAPIDS: This was a real natural name for this fishing spot. The rapids really did sound like thunder as you approached it from upstream. There is always a mist in the air above most of these rapids. Probably from the ice cold water, falling to the next level and the warmer air above it.

The weathermen name their hurricanes after women and our fishermen normally name their favorite fishing holes after women.